SUPER SIMPLE
PAPER AIRPLANES

SUPER SIMPLE
PAPER AIRPLANES

Nick Robinson

STERLING

New York / London
www.sterlingpublishing.com

STERLING and the distinctive Sterling logo are registered trademarks
of Sterling Publishing Co., Inc.

2   4   6   8   10   9   7   5   3   1

First published in the U.S. in 2000 by Sterling Publishing Co., Inc.
This edition published in 2009 by Sterling Publishing Co., Inc.
387 Park Avenue South, New York, NY 10016
© MCMXCI Quintet Publishing Ltd

Published in Great Britain by Quantum Publishing
6 Blundell Street, London N7 9BH, UK

Distributed in Canada by Sterling Publishing
c/o Canadian Manda Group. 165 Dufferin Street
Toronto, Ontario, Canada M6K 3H6

For information about custom editions, special sales, premium and
corporate purchases, please contact Sterling Special Sales
Department at 800-805-5489 or specialsales@sterlingpub.com.

Manufactured in Singapore

Sterling ISBN 978-1-4027-7026-5

CONTENTS

INTRODUCTION

Man's desire to fly dates back to the earliest times, from the legendary Icarus and the 18th-century efforts of the Montgolfier Brothers, right up to the fateful Thursday in 1903 when Wilbur and Orville Wright made the first heavier-than-air flight.

Nowadays, we take it for granted when aircraft fly at several times the speed of sound with a computer in control, performing the most amazing acrobatics. Yet, deep within us, there is still a fascination with all things that are able to leave the earth behind. Few of us have been able to watch swallows swoop and dive in the evening sun without feeling a touch of envy.

This longing may be one cause of our love-affair with paper airplanes. The traditional dart is probably the most folded design on earth. Many hundreds of thousands must have been made over the years by eager schoolchildren and by adults with a little time to spare.

No one knows exactly how old the concept of a paper plane is, but it is probably a 20th-century innovation. The folding of paper aircraft has close links with the art of origami (which literally means "folding paper"). The growth of interest in paper flight in the 1960s was probably an offshoot of the great technical and artistic advances made in origami during that period.

Most of the designs in this book have been created by people who are primarily paper-folders rather than aircraft enthusiasts, but the appeal of paper aircraft transcends the appeal of origami. Perhaps this is because paper aircraft remind us of the carefree days of our youth, and the thrill of sending a dart higher and further than anyone else. Despite its apparently trivial nature, creating paper aircraft can be an exacting and time-consuming activity. The designers of sophisticated aircraft know of the value of simple aerodynamics, as displayed by a paper dart.

This book is aimed at anyone who has ever wanted to try their hand at tried and tested paper aircraft, and it also includes one or two rather unorthodox designs. No previous folding experience is needed. After trying these examples, I hope you will feel inspired not only to create your own designs, but to try other subjects and discover the true and lasting joy of paper-folding.

NICK ROBINSON

CHAPTER 1

THE BASICS OF FOLDING

PAPER

Paper is composed of fibers of wood, held together with a special type of glue called "sizing". When you gently bend the paper, the fibers are able to flex and return to their original position. When you make a crease in the paper, the fibers are bent so much that they stay in their new position. This means that paper-folders must always be accurate. The paper "remembers" wrong creases just as well as it does correct ones! Accuracy is especially important when making paper airplanes, as poor folding will probably mean poor flying.

The ability of the paper to remember a crease depends on both the composition and the thickness of the paper. We need to choose a type of paper that will be strong, yet light. This will allow us to fold planes that are rigid enough to cope with crash landings yet not so heavy as to be difficult to fly.

If we are folding from squares, another important factor is the grain. When paper is made, the fibers of wood tend to line up in a certain direction, known as the "grain". This makes the paper easier to fold in one direction (with the grain) than the other (against the grain). You can determine the direction of grain by the following procedure. Place the paper flat on the palms of your hands and gently flex the sides upward and inward. Feel the tension in the paper, and note how much it resists the pressure of your hands. Now turn the paper around so

the next side faces toward you and repeat the process. You should be able to detect a distinct difference between the two. If the paper flexes easily, the grain is running in aline away from you. If the paper has more resistance, the grain runs from side to side.

More resistance: grain runs horizontally   Less resistance: grain runs vertically

We can make use of the grain to stiffen the wings by folding so that the grain runs from side to side on the finished design. If the wing creases run with the grain, they will tend to flop up and down more easily. When starting a design, look ahead on the diagrams to determine which sides represent the wings. Then turn the paper so that the grain runs across from wing to wing. This theory is easy to apply with square paper, but with rectangular paper it will of course be a matter of luck if the grain runs in the ideal way.

There is a maximum size beyond which paper airplanes won't fly. This is because, at a certain point the weight of the paper becomes so great that the wings won't hold their shape and angle.

Standard letter-size paper is usually the best, and is certainly the most popular size. Experiment with different makes and types to find the most suitable.

More information on paper is given in chapter two.

HOW TO FOLD

Folding on a flat surface (such as a table or book) is certainly the easiest method. You will find by experience that certain folds are easier if you hold the paper in the air, but the majority will be more accurately folded on a table. Find a clear space where you can lay out this book and a few sheets of paper. If there are small bits of rubbish on the table, they may interfere with your creasing.

Few activities can be performed well if they are rushed and this is especially true of paper-folding. Choose a time when you have some peace and quiet and don't rush the folds. Once you have mastered a particular design you will find it becomes easier and easier to make, but you will still need to concentrate to get the best results. It also helps to have clean hands.

Start with a rectangle in front of you. Turn it so a long side is toward you and fold it away from you to the opposite side. Do not flatten yet. Try to keep the lower side of the paper still, and line up the upper half with it. It is a good idea to move slightly past the lower edge, then slightly back from it and repeat, making smaller movements each time. Stop when you are sure that the edges are together.

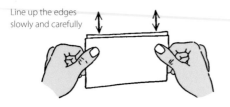
Line up the edges slowly and carefully

Once in position, move one hand on to the paper somewhere near the two edges, holding the paper so that it can't move. Now press the first finger of the other hand in the ward of the paper and slide it back toward you until it touches the folded edge. Flatten the paper by sliding your finger first to one side, then back to the other. Check that the two edges are still neatly lined up, then reinforce the crease by pressing it firmly along the edge.

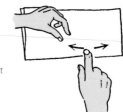
Hold in place whilst flattening

Try to concentrate the pressure on the tips of your fingers, not the sides or the heels of your hand, which are less effective. Some people try to flatten creases with their teeth, but this weakens the paper and there is a danger of cutting your tongue! Always fold slowly; even when you have mastered the basic technique of folding, you should always take your time and be as neat as possible.

TYPES OF CREASE

There are only two types of crease in origami and you make them both every time you fold a piece of paper. Even the most complex airplane ever designed is made up of the two basic creases. After making a fold, open the paper, without flattening it, and look at the crease. The crease goes into the paper, forming a dent. In origami, this is called a VALLEY crease. Turn the paper upside down and you find the crease comes out of the paper slightly, forming a bump or MOUNTAIN crease. just as in nature you cannot have mountains without valleys, so it is with paper-folding; you cannot make a valley crease without forming a mountain crease at the same time.

SYMBOLS

The distinction between valley and mountain creases is central to folding so we use special symbols to show which is which. These were first invented by the Japanese Master, Akira Yoshizawa, and have been accepted as a world-wide standard.

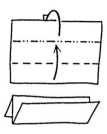

Mountain & valley (note different arrowheads)

A valley crease means fold the paper onto the facing side. The symbol is always a series of dashes and the arrowhead is the conventional type. A mountain crease means fold the paper onto the opposite side and the arrowhead is only on one side of the arrow.

Turn over (note earlier creases on the paper). Dotted lines show x-ray view

Watch out for the turn over symbols – they are very important and easily missed. You should turn the paper over from side to side as if you are turning over a page of a book. The thin line indicates a crease previously made. The dotted lines show an x-ray view to help you see where the hidden paper lies.

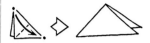

Fold dot to dot; the next drawing is larger

Dots are often used to show precise location points. If the next drawing is appreciably larger, yet another type of arrowhead will show this.

Fold and unfold, equal distances

An arrow that goes across the paper and returns means you should make the fold, crease firmly and then unfold to the original position. The ruled line will indicate where equal distances apply, such as in half, in quarters etc.

Equal angles

Equal angle signs show where a corner is bisected by the fold. These signs are used to reinforce the usual instructions.

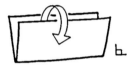

Unfold or pull out, in this case to right angles

A solid arrow shows that you should unfold the paper or pull out a hidden flap or layer. Where this means unfold to right angles (such as for a wing), a small right-angle sign is added.

Press or apply pressure; rotate the paper

A black triangle means you press the paper or generally apply pressure (gently!). Two rounded arrows indicate the paper should be rotated in the direction of the arrows, usually by 90 degrees.

Repeat arrow

An arrow with notches on it shows that the fold you have just made should be repeated elsewhere. The number of notches shows the number of repeats (in this case, two).

THE REVERSE FOLD

A technique which might at first seem unusual is the reverse fold. This is commonly used to turn part of the body section of the airplane into a tail-fin. The paper may fold between two layers (inside reverse fold) or less commonly outside them (outside reverse fold). Here is the symbol and method for an inside reverse fold.

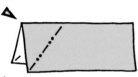

1 The symbol for an inside reverse fold.

2 Valley and unfold. The secret is to make the crease very sharp.

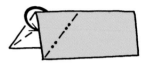

3 Start to push the top corner inside the tent-like shape. The name "reverse" comes from the fact that a section of the top crease reverses from mountain to valley.

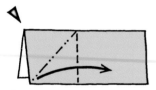

4 Like this. Keep pushing the paper carefully inside. If it starts to crumple, open out, flatten the paper and start again, carefully.

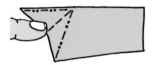

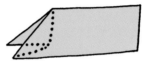

5 The paper will flatten to this position, the dotted lines show an x-ray view.

THE SQUASH FOLD

Similar to the reverse, the squash fold is done like this.

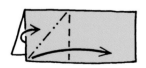

1 The symbol for the squash fold.

2 Valley and unfold, creasing sharply.

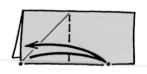

3 Again, crease and unfold.

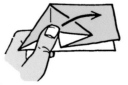

4 Start to refold the last crease, changing the diagonal to a mountain crease.

5 As the corner changes into a triangle, gently flatten it.

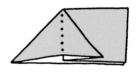

6 Complete. The dotted line shows the inside edge.

THE RABBIT'S EAR

This frequently used technique consists of four creases that are made simultaneously, as follows.

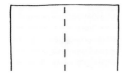

1 The symbol for the rabbit's ear.

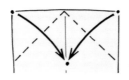

2 Creasing the first valley fold, only as far as the vertical crease (this will often be already present).

3 Repeat on the other side.

4 Fold on all three creases, pinching them together into a small upright flap.

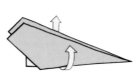

5 Flatten the flap to one side.

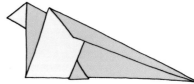

6 Finished.

Creases usually go from one edge of the paper to another edge, but sometimes you might need to crease only a part of the paper. Check carefully.

• Before you make a fold, always look at the next diagram to see how the paper will look when you have completed the fold.

• Always check the diagrams carefully and move the paper to make the fold as easy as possible. For instance with a mountain fold, turn the paper upside-down and make a valley fold. Don't forget to return it to the original position before continuing.

• The folds in this book are arranged roughly in order of difficulty within each chapter, so please try the designs in order unless you are an experienced folder. Moves that are explained in some detail early on will be described more briefly as you gain expertise. You will also find that you are asked in later designs to add the basic initial creases before the first step of the diagrams.

• Sometimes the paper can be so unhelpful you feel like throwing it in the nearest bin. This is a common reaction, so don't be discouraged — the paper will do as it's told, you have to ask it politely. It will then fly into the nearest bin!

• If your plane has a sharp nose, cut or tear it off — you don't want to be sued for poking out someone's eye!

• In nearly every case your initial attempts will be clumsy and probably won't fly very well. The second time you make a plane, the actual folds will be less of a problem and the result cleaner. In some cases it may take many attempts to produce a result that flies perfectly. The key to it all is to take your time and to keep adjusting the flying surfaces.

Happy flying!

CHAPTER 2

PAPER SIZES
AND TYPES

PAPER SIZES

The designs in this book are mostly made either from squares or from rectangles. The standard rectangle used throughout this book is equivalent to the American letter size 8½ x 11 in (210 x 295 mm) or European A4 size paper. Small adjustments to the flying surfaces will overcome most problems. Instructions are given to convert paper sizes if necessary.

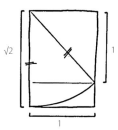

1:√2 proportions (a silver rectangle)

CONVERTING A RECTANGLE TO A SQUARE

Squares can be made by folding two adjacent sides of a rectangle together and cutting at right angles to the matching edges (see diagrams below). The more accurately the paper is cut, the easier it will be to fold neatly.

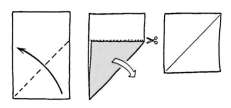

Making a square from a rectangle

CONVERTING TO A "SILVER" RECTANGLE

The 1:√2 rectangle is sometimes called the "silver" or "true" rectangle. It has a side that is the same length as the diagonal of an enclosed square (see diagram above). It has the fascinating property of retaining the same proportions when doubled or halved in size. The "A" sizes are rectangles of this type. Thus any design from a sheet of A4 can be made twice by halving the paper into A5 rectangles.

If you are starting with paper that is not in "A" proportions, and want to turn it into a silver rectangle, you can convert it by one of the following methods.

FROM A SQUARE

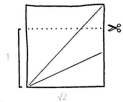

1 Crease a diagonal then fold the lower side to meet it.

2 Make a new crease, at right angles to vertical edges, just passing through the folded corner.

3 Remove the small section to leave a silver rectangle.

Converting from a long triangle to a 'silver' triangle

If your paper is too long, you can convert it into a silver rectangle as follows.

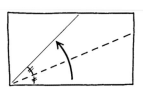

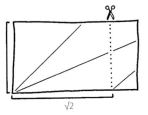

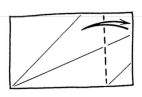

1 Again mark the diagonal and fold the edge to it.

2 Fold the small tip behind and back up again. Unfold the lower corner.

3 Fold the right side over so that the crease starts where the small crease meets the lower edge. unfold.

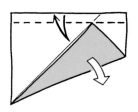

4 Remove the surplus.

Converting from a wide triangle to a 'silver' triangle

For a rectangle that is wider than a silver rectangle; repeat the method for a square above, removing the surplus paper.

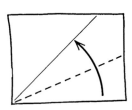

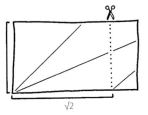

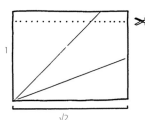

FROM PAPER 8½ X 11½ IN (21½ X 29 CM)

Remove ¾ in (2 cm) from one of the long sides. (Conversely, to convert A4 paper to 8½ x 11½ in (21½ x 29 cm) proportions, remove ⅞ in (2 cm) from one of the short sides.)

TYPES

There is an infinite variety of paper to choose from, and they differ in their weights, textures, wards, properties and thicknesses. Some are better suited to darts, some to gliders, some to spinning designs. The best way to find out is to experiment. The instructions for each design will give recommendations if a specific type of paper is best; otherwise it is up to you. Some designs will work very well out of foil-backed paper, whereas some delicate gliders may not fly at all made from that medium.

Most serious folders are constantly on the lookout for paper and will check out the most unlikely sources. There are certain beautifully decorated papers that only seem to be available from florists. Newsagents and art/craft stores are obvious places to start. The former will have many different patterns for wrapping presents and they are likely to be quite cheap. The latter will have a wider range but you may have to pay a little more. Don't feel you have to buy paper. Use anything you can lay your hands on – banknotes, cheques, leaflets, tickets, posters, handouts, anything (except tissue and newspaper)!

If you have an artist's folder, this is ideal for storing paper. Or a large drawer or box can be used. Try to store your paper flat whenever possible.

Once you have been bitten by the folding bug, you will become much more aware of paper and its properties, and will quickly recognize which types of paper will suit which designs.

CHAPTER 3

PRINCIPLES OF FLIGHT

The first theories of flight were proposed by a scientist, Sir George Cayley, nearly a hundred years before man actually flew in a heavier-than-air machine. These theories were put into practice by the Wright Brothers at the turn of the century and are still applied in the design of modern aircraft. The same principles determine whether or not a humble paper airplane will fly.

RESISTANCE

We shall start by making a simple "design" to illustrate the theory. Hold a rectangular sheet of paper by the short end at arm's length, then let it drop to the floor. Note how long it takes and the way it swirls around unpredictably. Take another sheet, crumple it up firmly into a ball and then drop it alongside the first sheet.

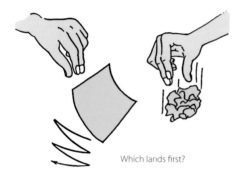

Which lands first?

The ball will hit the floor before the sheet because, being smaller, it meets less air resistance.

Resistance is the pressure you feel if you try to walk into a strong wind. However, you can easily prove that even still air offers resistance. Put a sheet of paper on the palm of your hand, quickly turn it into the vertical and spin round in a circle.

The paper stays pressed against your hand by the resistance of the air. If you slow down, the paper will fall to the floor because the amount of resistance is related to how fast the object is through the air, properly known as air speed.

DRAG

As well as the airspeed, another factor that affects resistance is the shape of the object; a small rounded shape will cause less resistance than a large angular one. This can be seen in the design of most vehicles. Sports cars, designed to go fast, always have a smooth streamlined shape. Lorries, designed to carry weight, are usually rectangular and are consequently much slower.

Related to the resistance caused by an object is the amount of turbulence caused behind it. Air behaves in a similar way to water – the twists and eddies in the air behind a plane are like those in the water behind a boat, except that we can't usually see them. A streamlined shape will slip easily through water or air and cause little turbulence behind it. A more bulky shape may be held back by an excess amount of turbulence.

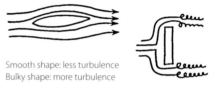

Smooth shape: less turbulence
Bulky shape: more turbulence

When engineers are designing new airplanes, they use smoke in a wind tunnel to see where the turbulence is and whether modifications will reduce or increase it. Since a plane needs to slice smoothly through the air, we need to reduce both resistance and turbulence (which combine to produce drag) as much as possible.

THRUST

Airplanes need huge engines and propellers to provide the thrust, but for paper versions the thrust comes from throwing. Perhaps throwing is too forceful a word, but it is usually the power of our arms and wrists that provides the forward thrust. One exception is the use of elastic bands for a couple of unusual designs in this book. Since we can only provide thrust at launching, the forward momentum will immediately begin to decrease and gravity will pull the plane down.

LIFT AND PRESSURE

Lift is the force that acts on the wing to move it upward and hence to keep a plane in the air. It is caused by having a greater air pressure under the wing than above it, so the wing tends to rise.

To see this in action, take a small strip of paper and hold it by the corners of the short end, just below your mouth. If you now blow across the upper surface, the paper will rise up, even though you are blowing down onto it! By blowing across the top, you in fact reduce the pressure there, rather than increase it as you might expect. How does this happen? The scientific answer is called Bernouilli's Principle. Put simply, the pressure of a gas (such as air) decreases as its speed increases and vice versa.

Imagine water flowing down a tunnel. If the tunnel gets narrower, the water must flow faster so that the same amount of water comes out as goes in, otherwise the tunnel would burst. If the tunnel narrows to half' its original width, the speed of water is doubled and the pressure is halved. A special type of tube called a venturi makes use of this principle in many commonplace applications, such as the carburettor of a car.

A Venturi Tube

We can demonstrate Bernouilli's Principle in other ways. Hold up two sheets of paper by their edges, with a gap of about 2 in (5 cm) between them. Blow between the sheets and see what happens. The same reaction causes a door that is slightly open to close when a draught passes through the gap.

Alternatively, take a strip of card and bend either end down to form a simple bridge. Place it on a table and blow underneath it. What happens? In both these cases, the increased airspeed through a narrow gap causes the pressure to lower and the paper to move toward the gap.

If the air is made to speed up, the same effect

Increased airspeed over the top of the wing means reduced pressure, causing lift

occurs, even if there is no gap. If we look at a wing in cross-section, the top half is generally curved. When the air flows past it, it is pressed upward over the curve, and so has to travel faster than it does over the relatively flat lower surface. As it travels faster, the pressure above is decreased relative to that below the wing and so the wing is forced upward.

Four factors act upon a plane in flight, be it

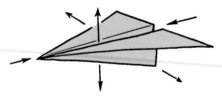

Increased airspeed over the top of the wing means reduced pressure, causing lift

made from steel or paper. Thrust impels the plane forward, whilst drag tends to slow it down again. Lift forces the plane up against the pull of gravity.

THE "QUICKIE"

Let's make a simple wing and see how aerodynamic forces act in practice. The design is by Charles Peck of the USA and is called the "Quickie" for obvious reasons! Start with the nearest handy rectangle.

Maximum drag is produced by air meeting a flat surface head-on. Minimum drag would be produced by making a piece of paper move through the air edgewise. This can easily be done by making one end heavier than the other.

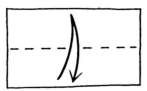

1 Fold a long edge to the opposite edge, crease and open.

2 Fold the same edge to the center crease.

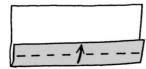

3 Fold the doubled section in half.

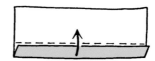

4 Fold the thick section over on the original center crease. Press the creases firmly to flatten them.

Hold the wing by the thin end with the thick end hanging down and release it. It will fall to the floor quickly because it hardly disturbs the air at all. We have reduced the drag, but it won't go far forward until we give it lift as well. To put this into practice, take your wing and scrape the top of the rear (or "trailing") edge between your first fingernail and thumb to make it curl upward slightly. This forms the paper airplane equivalent of an "elevator". Hold as before and release. instead of diving straight to the ground, the paper should make a slower, forward descent.

By curving the rear of the wing upward, we have made an obstruction to the air, so the end of the plane is forced down. This counterbalances the extra weight at the front end, and should keep the plane more level in flight. If it dives to the ground, it is nose-heavy and needs a more curved elevator. if it climbs and dives alternately, it needs less. Keep adjusting until you get a steady path.

The distribution of weight is crucial to this balance. if the plane has more weight at the back, then the center of gravity (the physical point about which the plane balances) will be further back and the amount of lift needed to compensate will be beyond the ability of a simple paper aircraft. For this reason, the average paper airplane has the most weight concentrated at the front end.

The amount of lift required for a paper wing is actually very small because paper doesn't weigh very much and there is only a small force of gravity to be overcome.

With an elevator added, the 'Quickie' descends more gently

STABILITY

For a plane to be stable in flight, it should not move in any direction other than the one in which you launched it, except for a gradual descent. The three ways in which it could possibly turn are known as the longitudinal axis, the lateral axis and the directional axis. These axes are more commonly called pitch, roll and yaw.

Imagine your hand is a plane and hold it out, palm down, elbow bent. Pitching is when the nose goes up or down, as if your fingers move up and down. Rolling is when one wing goes up or down, as if you turn your thumb upward or downward. Yawing is when the plane turns to point in another direction, as if your elbow moves out or back.

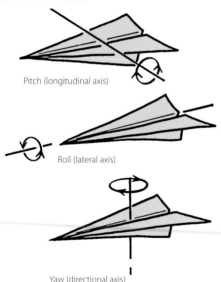

Pitch (longitudinal axis)

Roll (lateral axis)

Yaw (directional axis)

We made our Quickie wing more stable in pitch by adding an elevator. In more complex designs, the pitch stability is usually determined by the shape of the wings and the center of gravity, but we may add elevators as well.

We can reduce roll by adding what is known as dihedral angle.

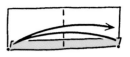

5 Make a gentle valley crease to raise the wings slightly, as in the profile.

With this improved design, if one wing starts to rise, the other has a greater surface area for the air to lift, so it will rise back and correct itself. On most paper aircraft it is easy to adjust the angle of the wings prior to flying.

The only remaining problem would be yawing, or veering off course. We can correct this by adding rudders to each wing.

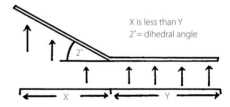

X is less than Y
2° = dihedral angle

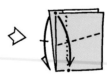

6 Fold the Quickie in half again.

7 Now fold the outside front corner of each wing to touch the folded edge at the point where the folded strip lies hidden within.

8 Open the wing out and adjust the angles of the folds as shown.

If you imagine the front view of the plane, the outside sections will be at their narrowest when the plane is going directly forward. If it starts to turn to one side, more rudder is exposed and the air pressure acts to straighten it again. Exactly the same principle applies to a ship's rudder. In most paper airplanes, the central keel of the plane acts as the rudder, and it operates in the same way. Launch the wing gently forward and it should have far more stability and perform well.

The main difference between real planes and paper ones is that we must set our elevators, dihedrals and rudders before launching and cannot alter them in flight to correct problems as a real pilot would. However, by adjusting them every time, it should be possible to make the wing (on any paper aircraft) fly straight and true.

LAUNCHING

The only other factor affecting the flight is how you launch the plane. Every design has a best speed and a best angle of launch. These two factors interact with each other and you can only find them by experimentation.

We are restricted in speed by the material we use. If you throw the plane too hard, the wings and flying surfaces will flex and bend out of shape, causing the plane to lose lift and stability before spiralling to the floor. If you launch it at too steep an angle, the resistance is so great that it overpowers the lift and the plane loses airspeed in what is known as a "stall". If your plane keeps going up and down in a roller-coaster fashion, it may be stalling. You are launching either too fast or at too steep an angle. Keep trying!

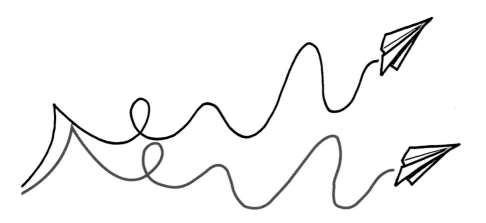

Roller-coasting is a sign you have launched the plane too fast or at too steep an angle.

CHAPTER 4

CLASSIC DESIGNS

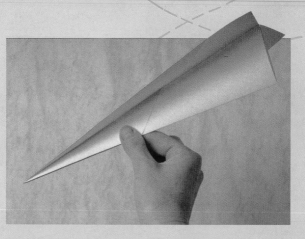

The designs in this chapter are of uncertain origin and have been classified as classic because they have been around for so long. Designs, in nature or origami, last only if they are both effective and efficient, and this is certainly true of the four designs in this chapter.

When folders learn how to make a paper airplane that seems to work very well and has a neat folding sequence, they are likely to remember it and to teach it to others. They in turn will pass the design on and eventually the design is known all over the world. Usually by this time the name of the creator has unfortunately been forgotten, but his creation lives on, and in time becomes a "classic".

Classic lines are invariably clean, and the folding sequence can be duplicated exactly every time you make them. Unlike some more complicated designs, where you need to adjust and balance various flying surfaces, these classic designs will work every time, as long as you fold carefully.

CLASSIC DART

This is without doubt the best known of all paper airplanes, probably because its simplicity and beauty have no equal. If you have never folded paper before, this is the best design to start with since it is almost impossible to get it wrong, providing you take your time. If you know how to make it, try to fold slowly and produce the neatest example you have ever made.

As with all airplanes that have a sharp nose, it is a good idea to cut a small section off to make it safe when throwing. The effect this has on the flight pattern will be negligible.

Start with a rectangle, colored side down. Fold in half width-wise and open.

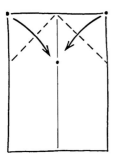

1 Lift each corner and fold it to meet the center crease. Make sure it lines up exactly.

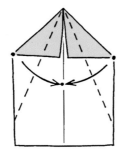

2 Narrow by taking the folded edges (made in step 1) to meet the center crease. Try to keep the upper point sharp.

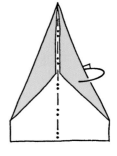

3 Mountain fold in half. You may find it easier to turn the paper over and make a valley fold.

4 Narrow still further by folding each of the two folded edges to the right hand vertical edge. Turn the paper round so it is horizontal.

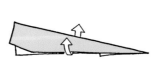

5 Open the wings up to 90 degrees.

FLYING HINTS
Launch the dart firmly at a slight upward angle. You may need to adjust the angle of the wings (dihedral) for the best results. Thrown properly, it will fly for more than 10 m (30 ft)

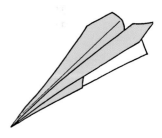

6 The Classic Dart finished.

CLASSIC GLIDER

The design of this plane is traditional, but the clever triangular "lock" was made popular by the eminent Japanese designer of paper airplanes, Eiji Nakamura.

Whereas the classic dart is designed for fast flight, this design concentrates a lot of layers at the front to provide weight and hence stability. Start with a sheet of A4, colored side down.

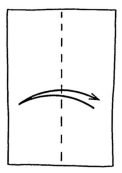

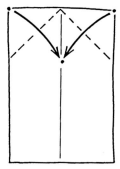

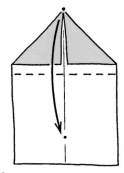

1 Fold the two long sides together, crease firmly and open to form the vertical center crease.

2 Fold two corners in to lie along the center crease. Try to make the edges lie exactly along the crease.

3 Bring the top corner downward to touch a point a short distance from the lower edge. Note that the valley crease does not lie along the inside edges formed in the last step.

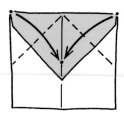

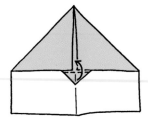

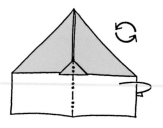

4 Repeat step 2 with the upper folded edge. The corners do not meet the inside corner, but leave a triangular flap sticking out.

5 Fold the small triangle upward to hold the two corners together. This stops these flaps from coming loose during flight.

6 Use the center crease to mountain fold the paper in half behind. You can fold this in the air, or turn the paper over on the table and make a valley fold. Rotate the paper to the position shown in the next step.

CLASSIC GLIDER

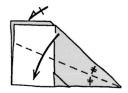

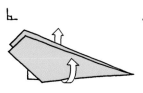

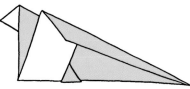

7 Fold the first upper flap downward to lie along the lower edge. Don't flatten until you are sure the edges are neatly lined up. Repeat on the other side.

8 Open out both wings to 90 degrees.

9 The Classic Glider ready for flight.

FLYING HINTS
Launch slowly and with moderate strength for a superbly stable flight-path. Alter the angle of the wings if it dives too quickly. Try different angles of attack for aerobatic stunts.

VIEW FROM BELOW

LAUNCHING POSITION

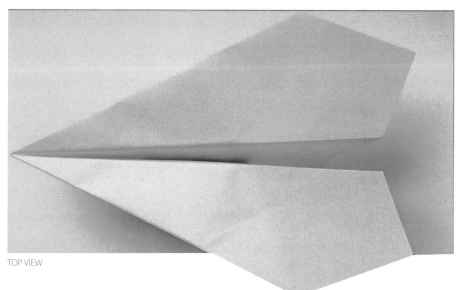

TOP VIEW

GLIDING TOY

This toy was first published in the 1970s, but nobody knows how old it is, or who invented it. Its beauty is in the simplicity of the design. You can fold it in a matter of seconds and it glides surprisingly well.

Start with a small square of light paper.

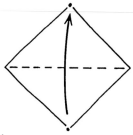

1 Fold in half from corner to corner.

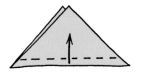

2 Fold a small strip over, try to make the crease parallel to the folded edge.

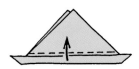

3 Fold the doubled strip over again.

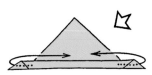

4 Bring the two strips around to meet each other. . .

5 . . .and tuck one inside the other. The further you can slide the strips into each other, the better the "lock" will be. Shape the ring; with your fingers to make it as circular as possible.

6 Complete.

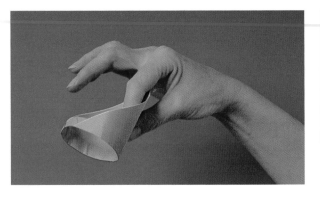

FLYING HINTS
Hold the tip of the tail with the first finger and thumb so that the loop is on top. Launch with a gentle push forward. The higher you are, the further it will travel.

HAWK DART

Apart from the classic dart, the hawk dart and its many variations is probably the best known of all paper airplanes. In origami terms, the techniques involved are quite sophisticated, but children of all ages seem to have no difficulty in making them. The formation of the nose produces a shape well-known in origami as a "fish base".

This design can be made from almost any shaped rectangle. Start with the colored side down, fold in half width-wise and open.

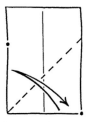

1 Fold the nearest short edge to the left hand edge, crease firmly and return.

2 Repeat to the right-hand side.

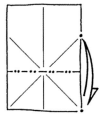

3 Add a mountain crease which passes through the intersection of the valley creases. (It is easiest to turn over and make a valley.)

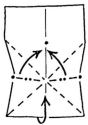

4 Press in the center of the creases. The sides of the mountain crease should "pop" upward. Using the creases you have made, swing the three lower dotted points toward the upper one.

5 This is the half-way stage.

6 Fold the loose point on either side down to the lower corner.

HAWK DART

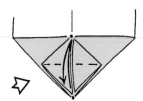

7 Pre-crease by folding the lower corner to the upper corner and return This is the first of three. creases that will form the nose of the plane.

8 Fold the upper left-hand edge to meet the center vertical edge return.

9 Repeat using the lower left hand edge.

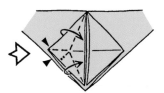

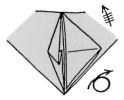

10 Start to fold in on the three valley creases, don't worry about the mountain yet. . .

11 Use thumb and first finger to shape the small triangular point, then flatten it toward you . .

12 Like this. Repeat steps 8 to 12 on the right-hand side. Turn the paper over.

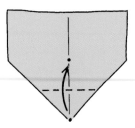

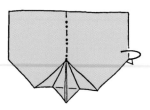

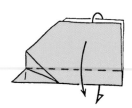

13 The horizontal crease is a mountain. Change it to a valley as you fold the lower corner in to reveal a kite shape.

14 Fold the right-hand side in half behind.

15 Using the top edge of the kite shape as a location, fold the wings down on either side.

HAWK DART

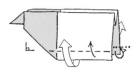

16 Make smaller 90 degree folds on the tips of either wing to form rudders, then open the wings out at right angles.

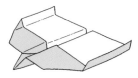

17 Finished.

FLYING HINTS
This is a very sturdy design, so you can launch it however you want — gently or hard. If you launch it forward it will glide smoothly, if you launch it high into the sky it will perform aerobatics. Experiment with rudder and wing angles.

CHAPTER 5

MODERN DESIGNS

All these airplanes have been designed within the last twenty years or so. In fact some could only have been designed recently since they use unusual origami techniques that were unknown twenty years ago.

Today's designers of paper airplanes may well have studied textbooks on aerodynamics and incorporated these principles into their work. Americans such as Collins, Weinstein and Weiss in particular have produced some remarkable and advanced work recently. This chapter represents a wide selection of the best modern paper airplane designs, arranged in order of complexity.

Some of the designs show a cross-fertilization of ideas and techniques. This is a normal and healthy practice providing influences are acknowledged. In other instances, creators will independently produce similar results using well-established techniques.

CANARD GLIDER

NICK ROBINSON

Back in 1902, Orville and Wilbur Wright made the first of many manned flights in the glider they designed and built themselves. The design they chose was known as the "Canard". The name comes from the French word for a wild duck and was chosen because of the location of stabilizers at the front end of the plane, reflecting the long neck of a duck in flight.

On this design, the traditional dart has been given a pair of horizontal stabilising fins at the front end, allowing more lift to be created. Subtle variations of the angle of each fin allows for many different flight patterns.

Start with a square of paper, colored side toward you. Fold in half, open and turn the crease so it is vertical.

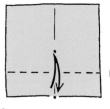

1 Fold in half, but only make a small location crease (or "pinch mark") before unfolding.

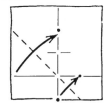

2 Fold the lower side to the pinch mark, crease and return. Turn the paper over.

3 Following the location points, fold the left-hand corner over and line up the creases — use the next diagram to help.

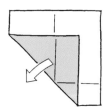

4 This is the result. Unfold the corner.

TOP VIEW

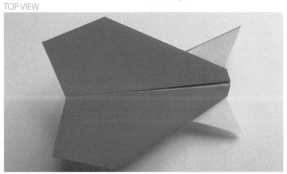

VIEW FROM BELOW

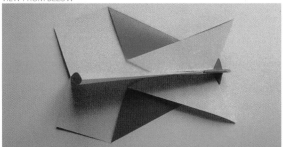

CANARD GLIDER

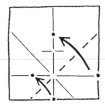

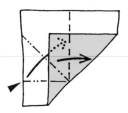

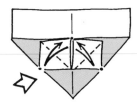

5 Make the same fold on the right-hand corner, but do not unfold.

6 Follow the creases carefully and re-position the lower quarter of the paper. The move should happen easily if your creasing was accurate. Use the next diagram to help.

7 Make the small pre-creases shown.

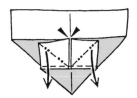

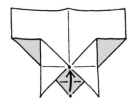

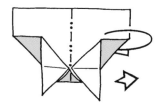

8 Turn the valley crease of the last step into a mountain. Add a horizontal valley crease as a "hinge" and fold the corner down, pressing the paper into a small triangle. Repeat on the other side.

9 This is the result. Fold over the small corner.

10 Swing the right-hand side around and behind.

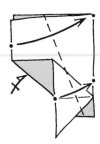

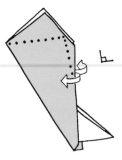

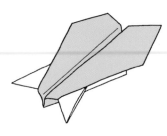

11 Fold both upper flaps over, carefully lining up the location points . . .

12 . . . like this. Crease firmly and open out each wing to 90 degrees.

13 The Canard finished.

CANARD GLIDER

FLYING HINTS
Initially, keep the front fins
slightly above the angle of the
wings, then adjust as necessary
to obtain a balanced flight.
Launch with a gentle push, with
a slight angle of attack.

REEVE'S FLOATER

MARK KENNEDY

This simple design was created especially for a young friend of Mark's and was tested from way up in a New York skyscraper. Try to use some colorful paper that is fairly stiff for the best results. Start with a sheet of A4, color down, and fold in half both ways. Turn the long side toward you.

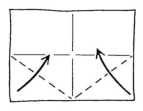

1 Make two folds that join up the nearest halfway point with the center points of the short sides.

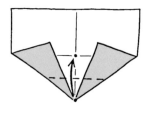

2 Fold the new corner to the center point.

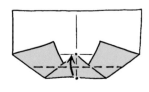

3 Take the lower folded edge to the center horizontal crease.

4 Swing the narrow strip over using the horizontal center crease. Flatten the paper firmly.

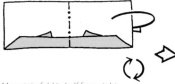

5 Mountain fold in half from right to left and turn the paper round 90 degrees.

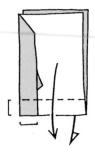

6 Enlarged view. Note the approximate distances shown and fold each wing downward.

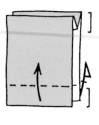

7 Fold the tips of each wing up by the same amount as the last step.

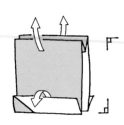

8 Open the wings and wingtips out to 90 degrees.

REEVES FLOATER

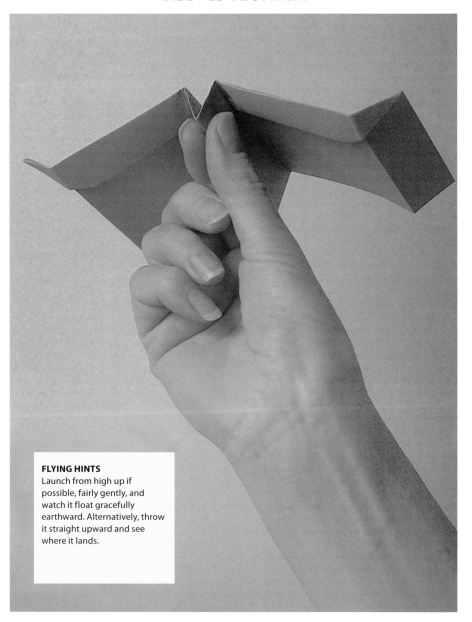

FLYING HINTS
Launch from high up if
possible, fairly gently, and
watch it float gracefully
earthward. Alternatively, throw
it straight upward and see
where it lands.

JS DART

JOHN SMITH

John Smith is a folder who applies what some might consider severe restrictions to many of his designs. They must come from a square and must only consist of valley and mountain creases. He has named this approach "pureland" and has developed several interesting techniques to replace complicated squash or reverse folds.

Special care must be taken when folding this airplane to ensure the nose is neat and sharp. The finish of the underside is particularly elegant and attractive.

Start with a square, colored side down. Fold in half from corner to corner and turn the paper so the crease points away from you.

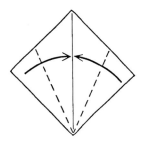

1 Fold both lower sides to meet the center crease.

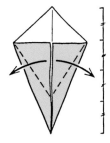

2 Fold the paper in half from top to bottom, making a very gentle pinch. This locates the ¼ mark. Starting from this point, fold the two inner corners back out as far as they will go.

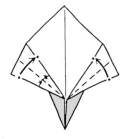

3 Fold the lower raw edges in to lie on the inside folded edges. Be accurate.

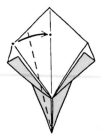

4 Fold the left-hand side in to meet the center crease, bisecting the angle.

5 Starting at ¼ mark again, fold the flap back out as far as it will go. This move is similar to step 2.

6 This is the result. Repeat the last two steps on the right-hand side.

JS DART

LAUNCHING
POSITION

VIEW FROM BELOW

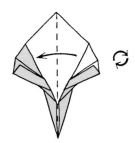

7 Valley fold the plane in half and turn it to point to the left.

8 Make a crease that bisects the body of the plane, taking the upper edge to the lower. Take your time and try to be as neat as possible. Open the wings back out to 90 degrees.

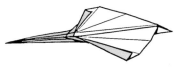

9 The finished JS Dart.

FLYING HINTS
When launching this design, take extra care that there are no people in front of you since the sharp nose could cause injury. Launch quite gently.

STUNT PLANE

MAX HULME

This design is the most acrobatic of all the airplanes in this book. It is ideal for paper-folders who are stuck in a hospital bed, because it will come back to you! Neat curling of the wingtips requires a bit of practice, but the results are well worth it. The blunted nose of the Stunt Plane means you can throw it very hard without worrying about hitting anyone.

Start with a square, colored side down, creased along the center.

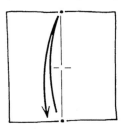

1 Gently pinch the half-way point of the central crease.

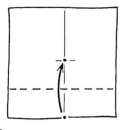

2 Fold one end of the crease to the center.

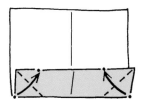

3 Fold in each corner of the double layer to lie along the inside edge.

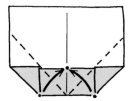

4 Valley in either side to lie along the vertical center crease.

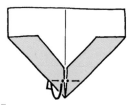

5 Mountain fold the tip behind to meet the original center pinch.

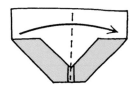

6 Fold in half from left to right.

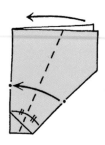

7 Enlarged view. Take the folded edge of the wing to meet the vertical edge. Line it up carefully and flatten well. Repeat behind.

8 Open the wings out to right angles. The trailing tips of the wings need to be curled upward by scraping them with your fingernail or by pulling them over a sharp edge.

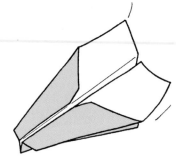

9 Ready for action.

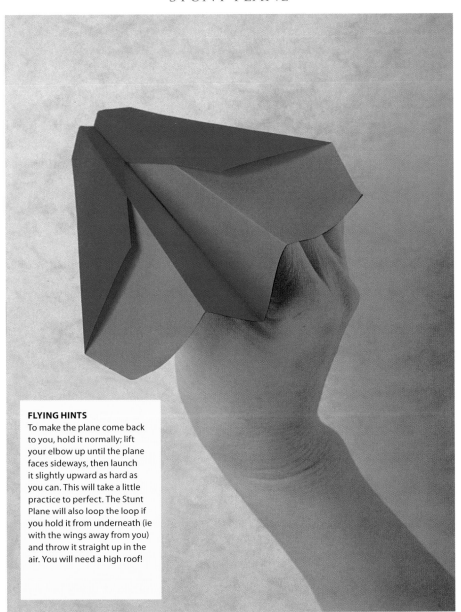

FLYING HINTS
To make the plane come back to you, hold it normally; lift your elbow up until the plane faces sideways, then launch it slightly upward as hard as you can. This will take a little practice to perfect. The Stunt Plane will also loop the loop if you hold it from underneath (ie with the wings away from you) and throw it straight up in the air. You will need a high roof!

BOMBER

Whilst having elegant and simple lines, this design has a rather complicated folding sequence and should be attempted only after you have tried a few of the simpler planes. I have named it "bomber" not because it carries bombs, but because the profile resembles one.

Start with a sheet of A4, colored side down. Make a long vertical center crease.

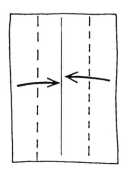

1 Fold both long edges to the center crease.

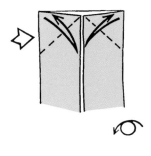

2 Fold both corners at one end to the center and return. Turn over.

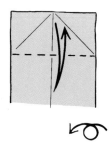

3 Add a valley crease using the locations shown and turn back over.

4 On the left-hand side, use established creases to swing the corner within the paper; the dotted lines in step 5 show the finished position. On the right-hand side, inside reverse the triangle. Turn the paper horizontally.

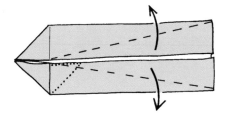

5 Fold either flap out as far as they will go from the starting point on the left, making sure the crease meets the right-hand corners neatly.

BOMBER

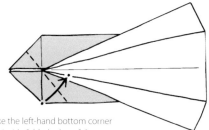

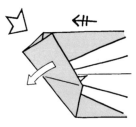

6 Take the left-hand bottom corner to the inside folded edge of the wing . . .

7 . . . like this. Crease firmly and return. Repeat on the upper side.

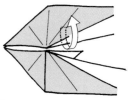

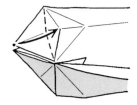

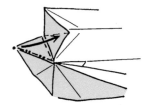

8 Lift up the layer to open a "pocket". The paper is not flat at this stage.

9 Swing the first corner inward on an established crease.

10 Swing the second corner in as well. The near-side edge will rise slightly. The paper is still three-dimensional.

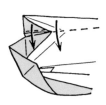

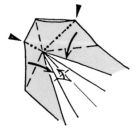

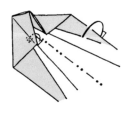

11 Lock the paper together by folding the top corner within on the crease shown.

12 Use the established crease to collapse the paper into a small tent-like flap. Fold over the tip of the small flap lying along the center crease (optional).

13 Fold the small flap inside a pocket on the left-hand side to help hold the layers together (optional). Mountain fold the plane in half behind.

BOMBER

TOP VIEW

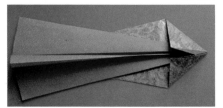

VIEW FROM BELOW   LAUNCHING POSITION

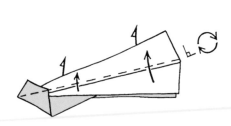

14 Following the inside edge of the wing, fold the wings over and open to 90 degrees on either side. Turn the paper over for . . .

FLYING HINTS
Stretch your arm back behind your head and launch the bomber into the air at a slight upward angle. Try not to throw too fast, but put plenty of power into it.

15 . . . the finished Bomber.

SNUB-NOSED DELTA

This is a variation on the Hawk Dart which avoids the more difficult folds on the nose cone and has beautifully clean lines. The lock that holds the nose together is simple yet effective. This design can also be made from almost any shaped rectangle. It is thought to have originated in Japan.

Starting with the colored side down, fold in half width-wise and open.

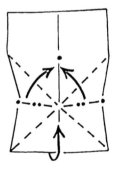

1 Fold the nearest short edge to the left-hand edge, crease firmly and return.

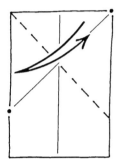

2 Repeat to the right-hand side.

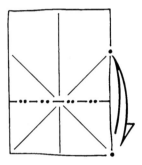

3 Add a mountain crease which passes through the intersection of the valley creases. (it is easiest to turn over and make a valley.)

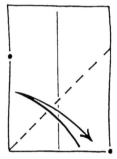

4 Press in the center of the creases; the sides of the mountain crease should "pop" upward. Using the creases you have made, swing the three lower dotted points toward the upper one.

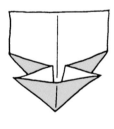

5 This is the half-way stage.

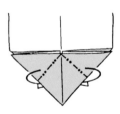

6 Mountain fold the loose point on either side behind to touch the bottom corner.

SNUB-NOSED DELTA

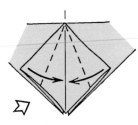

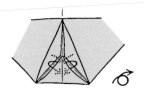

7 Enlarged view. Fold the upper edges of the square shape to line up with the center crease, forming an upside down kite shape.

8 Fold the lower triangle upward over the folded edges.

9 Bring the hidden corners out and tuck them into either of the two small pockets on the sides of the triangle. Turn the paper over.

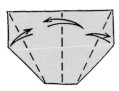

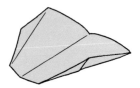

10 Make two creases joining the lower corners with the upper corners and reinforce the central crease as a valley. Adjust these creases to match the profile.

11 Finished.

12 Front view of the finished craft.

FLYING HINTS

The difficult part is actually holding the paper. Try to hold it by the two edges of the kite shape underneath, but don't hold it so tightly that the paper starts to buckle. The glider will fly long distances and is very well-balanced.

BACKWARDS PLANE

CARLOS GONZALEZ GARCIA

Many paper airplanes can loop the loop or perform stunts, but few of them can fly backward. The effect is, of course, an illusion. The profile of the design makes it look as if it is flying backward, but it is fun to give it to someone else and watch them try to launch it! The slightly tricky locking manoeuvre in step 9 can be avoided if you wish, but please – try it first.

Start with a square of medium-weight paper, colored side up, and crease both diagonals.

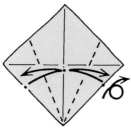

1 Fold two adjacent edges to the center crease and return. Turn the paper over.

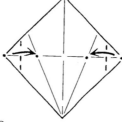

2 Fold the two outside corners to the intersection of the creases.

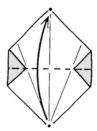

3 Fold in half upward.

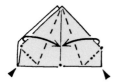

4 Using the long valley creases, fold the upper layer on either side to the center, neatly squashing the lower corners flat . . .

5 . . . into this position. Swing the central flap downward.

6 Pre-crease the lower point along the edge underneath.

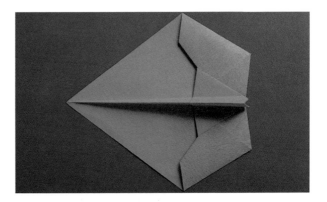

BACKWARDS PLANE

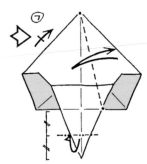

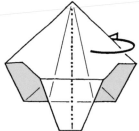

7 Mountain fold the lower point in half behind. Note the location points carefully, then make two pre-creases to form the wings.

8 Mountain fold in half from right to left.

9 You have two options here. The easy one is to keep the paper flat and simply tuck the lower flap within a pocket using the crease made in step 6 as a mountain. To get a better lock, hold the paper in your hand and open up the small pocket at the front of the right-hand wing (or the left, it doesn't matter). Use a finger to push/squeeze the flap within the pocket. This is a bit messy, but you can flatten the paper afterward. Use your finger or a small object to press the paper fully inside. This makes a very effective lock.

FLYING HINTS
The locked nose makes the airplane fly better, but it is by nature an unstable design. No matter how you launch it, it will do as it wants – sometimes looping, sometimes gliding. The novelty value outweighs this slight problem!

10 Open the wings out to right-angles.

11 Congratulations!

FOLD YOUR OWN

NICK ROBINSON

This simple design was developed from a dollar-bill design by Stephen Weiss and is intended to be made from a piece of cigarette paper. This is not a justification for the habit of smoking, but one packet will provide lots and lots of little gliders, all neatly creased in half and ready for folding!

The title comes from a well-known expression amongst low-Widget smokers.

Start with a sheet of cigarette paper (the design won't work with normal paper). Turn it so the side with the gummed strip is on the lower edge of the upper side.

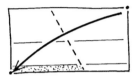 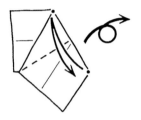 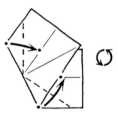

1 Fold the top right corner to the bottom left, licking and sticking the dotted area.

2 Take one end of the folded edge to the other, crease and return. Turn the paper over.

3 Fold both ends of the folded edge to meet the original halfway crease. Turn the paper slightly...

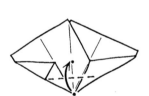

4 ...to this position. Fold the lower corner to touch the approximate center of the crease.

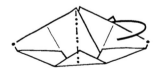

5 Fold in half behind from right to left.

FOLD YOUR OWN

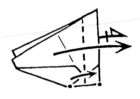  

6 Fold a wing to the right (the lowest edge folds in half). Repeat behind.

7 Crease the wings in half again, then open them out to match the profile.

8 Ready for flight.

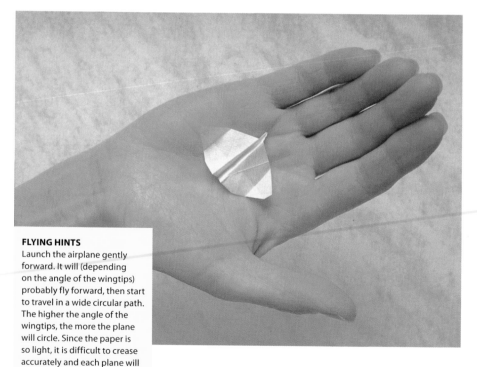

FLYING HINTS

Launch the airplane gently forward. It will (depending on the angle of the wingtips) probably fly forward, then start to travel in a wide circular path. The higher the angle of the wingtips, the more the plane will circle. Since the paper is so light, it is difficult to crease accurately and each plane will have its own flight pattern.

LEVEL-TRACK DELTA

STEPHEN WEISS

Stephen is an established origami author who has already produced a book on paper aircraft. This design first appeared in Flypaper, the American journal of paper flight, now sadly defunct. It is particularly stable in flight, hence the name.

Start with a sheet of American letter-size paper and fold the vertical center crease.

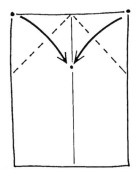

1 Fold the two upper corners to the center crease.

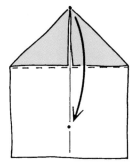

2 Swing the triangular section downward.

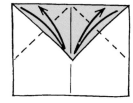

3 Repeat step 1 using the top folded edge, then unfold the corners.

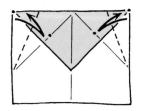

4 Fold each corner in so the outside edge lines up with the crease made in the last step, then unfold.

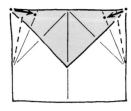

5 Again, fold in the edges to meet the most recent crease, but keep these folded.

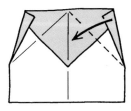

6 Fold in the right-hand corner on an established crease.

LEVEL-TRACK DELTA

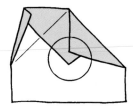

7 Here is the result; the circled area is enlarged in steps 8 and 10.

8 Fold the tip of the triangle underneath; the crease meets the corner.

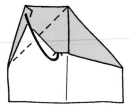

9 Fold the left-hand corner inward, ticking the small flap underneath the inner layer.

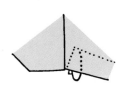

10 Pull out the right-hand small flap and tuck it underneath as well. This helps lock the paper together.

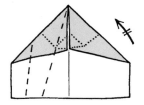

11 Make the creases shown. The inner one has location points, the outer one is made by eye. Repeat on the right-hand side (folding in half will make sure the outer creases match).

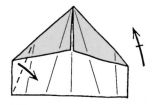

12 Make a crease that joins the lower corner with the top end of the outermost crease. Repeat on the right-hand side.

Profile of finished craft.

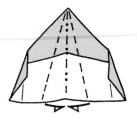

13 Form the paper into three dimensions using the central creases.

14 Fold the small flap in half outward, then make all the creases correspond to the profile shown.

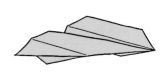

15 The Level-Track Delta.

LEVEL-TRACK DELTA

LAUNCHING POSITION

FLYING HINTS
Launch the plane at a moderate speed and it should fly very straight and level. If it climbs or dives, bend the middle of the trailing edges up or down slightly. Correct for turning by adjusting the symmetry of the wings.

VIEW FROM BELOW

TRI-PLANE

NICK ROBINSON

The "tri" in the name of this design refers not to the number of wings (there are two) but to the use of 60-degree geometry to produce a series of equilateral triangles. This is quite unusual; most paper airplanes are based around 45-degree creases, but a simple folding technique can also produce a perfect 60-degree angle. This is an area yet to be fully explored, so if you adapt this technique the chances are you will produce a truly unique design.

Start with a square, colored side down. Crease the vertical center crease and fold accurately.

Start with a sheet of cigarette paper (the design won't work with normal paper). Turn it so the side with the gummed strip is on the lower edge of the upper side.

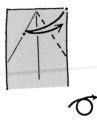

1 Fold either side to the vertical center crease.

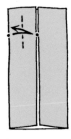

2 Make a location crease on the upper left-hand side, creasing quite gently and only where shown. Turn over..

3 Fold the upper left corner to touch the crease made in step 2, making sure the new crease starts at the center of the upper edge, then undo the fold.

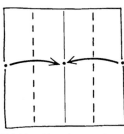

4 You have produced a 60-degree crease! Fold the right-hand corner across to line up with it, repeating the fold in step 3 and then unfold. Turn the paper over.

5 This is the crease pattern so far. Open out to a square again.

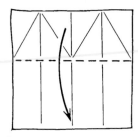

6 Using the 60-degree creases as guides, valley fold the upper edge downward.

TRI-PLANE

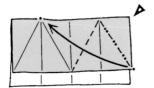

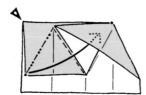

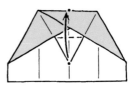

7 Use the creases to swing the right inside corner across to the upper left ¼ crease, pressing the small triangle flat as you do so. This is a very natural movement, but refer to the next diagram if you are unsure.

8 Repeat the move on the left, tucking the point within the pocket created in the last step.

9 Fold the internal (equilateral) triangle upward.

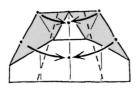

10 take both outer folded edges to the center crease, pressing firmly.

11 Mountain fold in half from right to left.

12 Open the wings out to right angles.

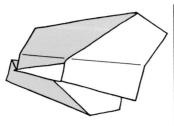

13 Finished.

VIEW FROM BELOW

FLYING HINTS
This is a stable glider, so launch in the normal way, checking the dihedral and the speed of launch to get the best results.

LAUNCHING POSITION

SKY YACHT

KUNIHIKO KASAHARA

This design by Kasahara doesn't look as if it will fly very well; there seems to be too much weight at the rear of the plane. However, when you try it, you will find out this is not the case. The central section or "sail" of the Sky Yacht makes it very eye-catching as it flies, so choose some decorative paper, or add your own designs to it.

Start with a square, colored side down. Add a diagonal crease.

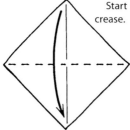

1 Fold in half from one end of the crease to the other.

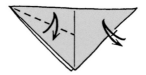

2 Fold one outer raw edge to the folded edge, but only crease as far as the vertical crease. Repeat on the other side.

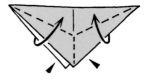

3 Use the creases you have just made along with the diagonal to raise the paper into a triangular flap . . .

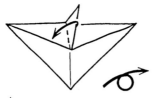

4 . . . like this. Flatten the flap to the left and turn it over.

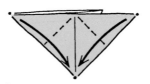

5 Take the two ends of the folded edge to the bottom corner of the triangle.

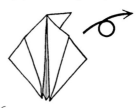

6 This is the result. Turn the paper over again.

7 Fold the upper edges of the square to the vertical center crease, allowing the flaps from beneath to swing out . . .

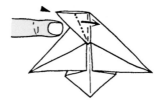

8 . . . The paper should now look like this. Squash the triangular flap evenly.

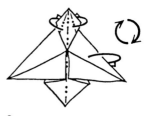

9 Fold the upper edges of the top point behind to leave a diamond shape, then fold the paper in half from right to left.

SKY YACHT

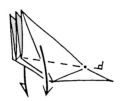

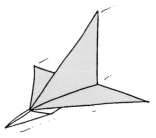

10 Unfold the rear corner to line up with the wings. Mountain fold the rear corners behind the wings.

11 Fold both wings down as far as they will easily go, then open them out to 90 degrees.

12 The Sky Yacht ready for sailing through the air.

Profile of finished Sky Yacht.

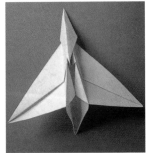

VIEW FROM BELOW

FLYING HINTS
Launch the plane as hard as you like, but make sure it is either level or pointing only slightly upward. It is stable, but does not produce much lift.

FLY DART

NICK ROBINSON

Paper insects that fly are hard to create. Insects are usually made of rounded shapes with thin legs, neither of which help paper versions to fly. It is possible, however, to combine some features of insects within designs that are more suited to

flying. This design incorporates the head of a fly. Although the body is too long for realism, the effect is undoubtedly "fly-like".

Start with a square, colored side down and crease along the vertical center.

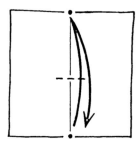

1 Fold in half, gently pinching the center-point.

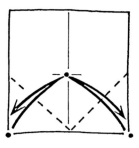

2 Take the two lower corners to the center and back in the familiar way.

3 Fold each half of the lower edge to meet the 45-degree creases made in the last step, then over again *on* those creases.

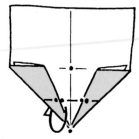

4 Mountain fold the lower corner behind to meet the center of the paper (located by the pinch mark in step I).

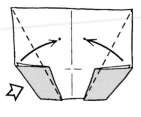

5 Noting the location points This is the result. Turn the paper over. carefully, fold each side in. Check the next diagram to help.

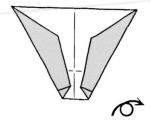

6 This is the result. Turn the paper over.

FLY DART

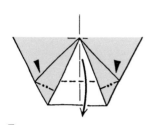

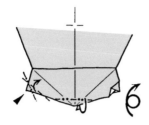

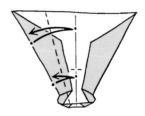

7 This is an enlarged view of the nose section. Put your thumbs underneath the triangular flaps and fold the upper corner downward as far as it will go. The flaps open out and squash in a new position, forming the mountain creases shown . . .

8 . . . like this. Fold the tip underneath, then form the eyes by folding the outer corners over and squashing the tips to the position on the right-hand side. Turn back over.

9 Fold the outer edge to the vertical center, crease firmly and return.

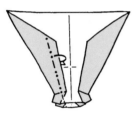

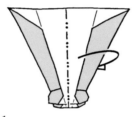

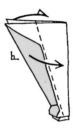

10 Turn the valley into a mountain and tuck the small flap underneath. Repeat steps 9 and 10 on the right-hand side.

11 Fold the right-hand side behind on the center crease.

12 Using established creases, open out the wings to 90 degrees.

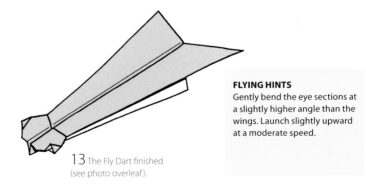

13 The Fly Dart finished (see photo overleaf).

FLYING HINTS
Gently bend the eye sections at a slightly higher angle than the wings. Launch slightly upward at a moderate speed.

FLY DART

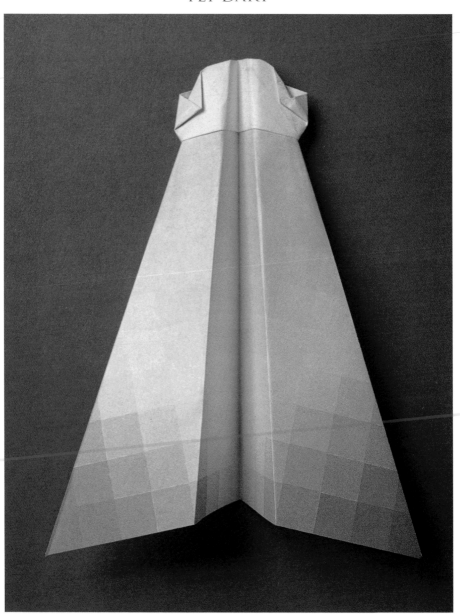

PARROT

EDWIN CORRIE AND NICK ROBINSON

This design is an excellent example of the cross-fertilization of ideas between designers of origami. The first nine steps are by Edwin Corde, the remainder by the author. The Japanese folder Kunihiko Kasahara has also produced a similar design.

The clean lines of the body are blended with the distinctive beak of a parrot to produce an interesting combination of bird and machine.

Start with a square, colored side down, creased in half both ways.

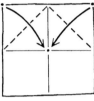

1 Fold two adjacent corners to the center.

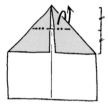

2 Fold the top corner behind to the center point and return.

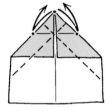

3 Fold the top corner to either end of the crease made in the last step.

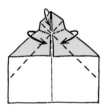

4 Use established creases to collapse the corner forward into a small square.

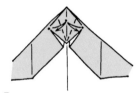

5 Fold the lower sides of the square neatly to the center and return.

6 Mountain fold the tip of the kite shape behind.

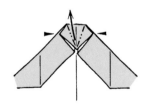

7 Lift the lower corner of the square upward, carefully flattening the sides inward . . .

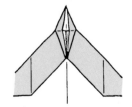

8 . . . like this. Press flat.

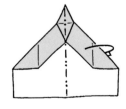

9 Take the right-hand side behind on the center crease.

PARROT

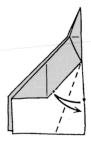 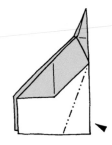 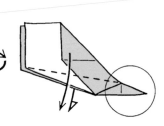

10 Take the vertical edge to the adjacent edge, crease firmly and return.

11 Sink the triangular section within the two layers.

12 Fold both wings downward. (The next three diagrams show the circled area enlarged.)

13 Pre-crease two 45-degree fold on the nose cone.

14 Outside-reverse fold on the inner creases.

15 Inside-reverse fold the tip of the beak.

 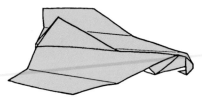

16 Add a shaping crease on either wing. Open the main wings out again and adjust the stabilizers to the angle shown.

17 Finished.

FLYING HINTS
If the bird has too much lift, flatten the stabilizers slightly. Launch with moderate strength.

PARROT

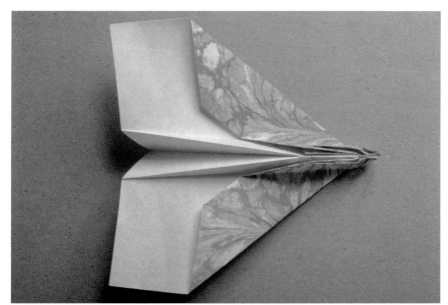

JET FIGHTER

KUNIHIKO KASAHARA

Kasahara is one of Japan's creative geniuses and has produced dozens of books about paper folding. He is a wonderful example to the rest of the origami world because he allows his folds to be published elsewhere, and he also uses other folders' work in his books, spreading the "sharing" gospel of origami. This airplane design is both simple and effective.

Start with a square, colored side down, with the center fold creased.

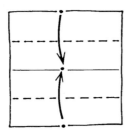

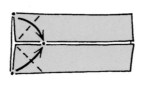

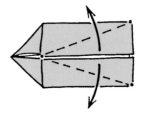

1 Fold opposite sides to the center crease.

2 Fold both corners of a short end to the center.

3 Make a crease that joins the inside corners from step 2 with the outside corners at the right-hand end,

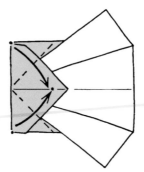

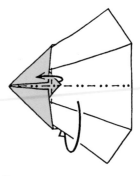

4 Valley the pointed flap inside, making the crease just right of the inside corners.

5 Enlarged view. Make creases from the front corner that pass through the intersection of the folded and raw edges. This may produce slightly varied results, depending where you made the last crease.

6 Fold the small triangle of paper on top of the corners (locking them in place), then mountain fold the paper in half.

JET FIGHTER

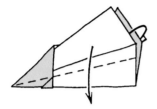 

7 Make a crease that starts at the pointed (nose) end and passes through the top of the small triangle. Fold both wings in this way.

8 Make a shaping crease along the inside folded edge, then open the wings out to right angles. Match the wings to the profile shown above.

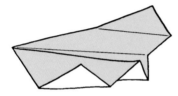

9 The completed Jet Fighter.

FLYING HINTS

Because there is quite a concentration of paper at the front end, you can launch the airplane as hard as you like. Try making the angle of the rudders uneven to make it curve. If you make one rudder point down, the plane will spin.

AVION

DIDIER BOURSIN

The Avion is a slow, graceful flyer and has a very steady flight-path due to the large wings. The large wing area lends itself to a crisp decorative paper. Fold carefully and try not to put any unwanted creases on the surface of the wings. This design is an object lesson in simplicity and balance.

Start with a square, colored side upward. Fold the vertical center crease.

1 Fold the two upper corners to lie along the center crease.

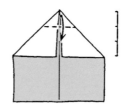

2 Fold the tip down about ⅓ of the way down the center edges.

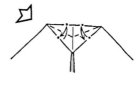

3 Enlarged view of the tip. Fold both inside edges of the small triangle to the upper edge, creasing only as far as the center.

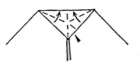

4 Use these creases to squeeze the triangle into a small point (known as a "rabbit's ear") then flatten this point to the right . . .

5 . . . like this. Turn the paper over.

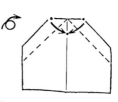

6 Fold the upper corners to lie along the center crease.

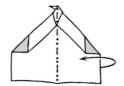

7 This is the result. Mountain fold the paper in half to the left.

AVION

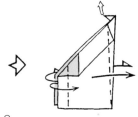 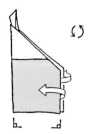 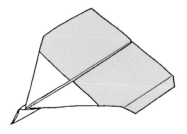

8 Pull out the hidden paper at the tip and make small valley folds at the edges of the wings (these form rudders). Fold both wings across at a shallow angle.

9 Open the wings out to right angles, the rudders to around 45 degrees, as shown in the profile.

10 L'avion c'est fini!

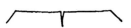

Profile of finished craft.

FLYING HINTS
Because the wings are so large, they are very prone to bending, so this plane flies best indoors away from strong air currents. Launch gently.

SWEPTBACK WING AIRPLANE

JAMES M SAKODA

This design is a modification of an original by Koso Uchiyama. Dr Sakoda won the First International Airplane contest in 1967 with his SST design. The sweptback wing can be made from either American-letter or A4 size, the only difference being the width of the tail section which is wider and slightly less elegant when made from A4. You may reduce this by trimming or folding.

The diagrams show A4 proportions, colored side down.

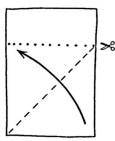

1 Fold the short edge to the left-hand long edge, then remove the remaining section as neatly as possible. This leaves a square folded diagonally.

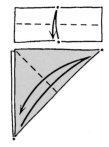

2 Fold the strip in half and unfold. Fold the triangle in half and unfold. Turn it so the folded edge is horizontal.

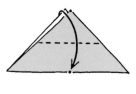

3 Fold the two loose corners in half downward.

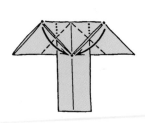

4 Slide the strip underneath the triangular flaps, then take the two upper corners to the lower point of the triangle.

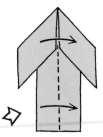

5 Fold in half from left to along the center crease.

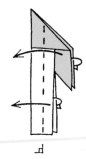

6 Fold both wings down, dividing the tail section in half. Open the wings to 90 degrees.

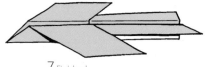

7 Finished.

SWEPTBACK WING AIRPLANE

FLYING HINTS
Launch the plane with moderate force. Make sure the raised section of the tailplane is at 90 degrees and not trailing down at all. You may improve lift by opening out the pockets under the wings slightly.

LITTLE NICK

NICK ROBINSON

This design utilizes both 45-and 60-degree geometry to produce a compact and highly effective performer. It employs the canard design to make the front end of the airplane more stable. "Little Nick" was created for my young son to be both visual and easy to launch.

Start with a square, preferably with highly contrasting colors, the main color upward. Add the vertical center crease.

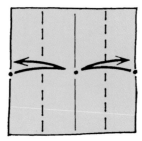

1 Add the quarter creases.

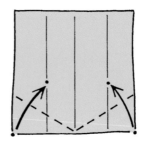

2 Starting at the center of the lower edge, fold either corner to touch the quarter creases. Be accurate! Turn the paper over.

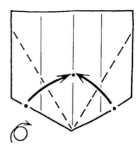

3 Take each folded edge to the center crease.

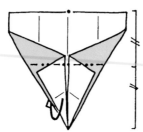

4 Mountain fold the lower point in half behind.

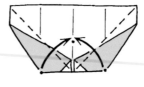

5 Fold each half of the lower folded edge to the vertical center crease.

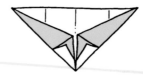

6 This is the result, turn the paper over.

LITTLE NICK

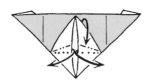 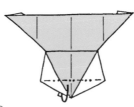 

7 Open the central edges, folding down on the (dotted) valley and flattening on the mountain creases . . .

8 . . . into this position. Fold the lower, corner behind along a hidden edge. If you wish, you can tuck this flap within the pocket there and then you can add the eyes of the "Fly Dart" should you wish to make it more menacing.

9 Fold in half from right to left.

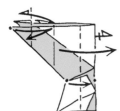 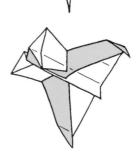

10 Pre-crease two outer ⅛ creases, then fold both wings over, noting the location points at the angle change.

11 Open both wings out and adjust to match the profile shown above right.

12 Complete.

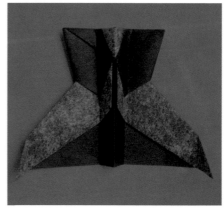

TOP VIEW

VIEW FROM BELOW

LITTLE NICK

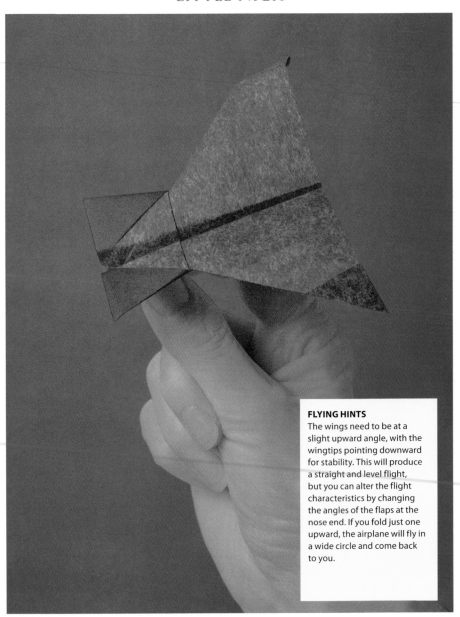

FLYING HINTS
The wings need to be at a slight upward angle, with the wingtips pointing downward for stability. This will produce a straight and level flight, but you can alter the flight characteristics by changing the angles of the flaps at the nose end. If you fold just one upward, the airplane will fly in a wide circle and come back to you.

BOXOID

MICHAEL WEINSTEIN

Looking at this design you might think it totally unique, but there are many origami designers who think along similar lines and discover nearly identical folds independently. London's Larry Hart created a "Box-glider" which only differs in a few respects.

This is a very mathematical design, so needs accurate folding. As the creator says, "once the flaps are locked in, nothing short of a thermonuclear detonation will pull them apart!"

Start with a sheet of A4, colored side down, and add the vertical center crease.

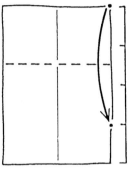

1 Locate the lower ¼ mark (see the JS Dart step 2) and fold the top edge to meet it.

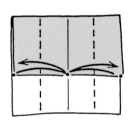

2 Fold either side to the center crease and return.

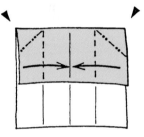

3 Perform two squash folds on either corner.

4 Unfold the two inner layers.

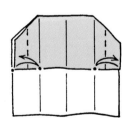

5 Fold the upper flaps in to the ¼ creases and return. These form the rudders in the final step. Turn the paper over.

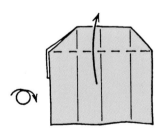

6 Fold the single layer upward.

BOXOID

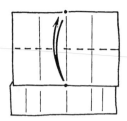

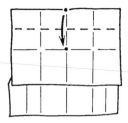

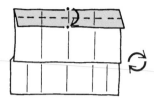

7 Fold the upper section in half and unfold again.

8 Take the upper edge to the crease you have just made.

9 Fold the double layer at the top inward in half.

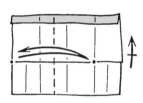

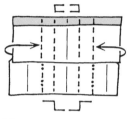

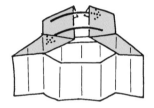

10 Take each outside edge to the opposite ¼ crease, adding ⅜th creases.

11 Study these creases very carefully before folding. The outside edges of the upper section swing inward to meet each other. The lower section however forms into a "step". The lines above and below show the final alignment.

12 In progress . . . When you know where the various flaps are going, tuck one inside the other as shown. It isn't important which side goes in which.

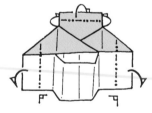

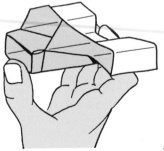

13 When the flaps are tucked in tightly (which isn't easy) lock the shape by folding the edge in, using an established crease. You have to hold the layers together whilst doing this and the paper will get crumpled slightly. Once it is all tucked in, you can flatten the layers again. Finally fold down the wingtips to the profile shown.

14 Ready for flight.

Profile of finished Boxoid.

BOXOID

TOP VIEW

VIEW FROM BELOW

FLYING HINTS

Because the nose of this design is quite heavy, you can launch it much faster than the average glider. Whilst it looks too "square" to fly properly, it is quite stable in flight and should travel for quite a long way. Depending on the size of your band (and the paper) you will hold it slightly differently. One way is to place your thumb at the front and two or three fingers at the rear, pushing it forward. Alternatively, hold either side with your thumb and three fingers, using your index finger to propel it. Experiment to find the most comfortable and successful method of launching.

LAUNCHING POSITION

GLIDER

FRANCIS OW

One of Singapore's premier folders, Francis is known for superb geometrical creations and has applied his knowledge of 60-degree geometry to produce this design. One or two of the moves are not immediately obvious, but if you fold carefully, all will be well. The glider begins its flight with a loop the loop!

Start with a square, colored side down, and make a vertical center crease.

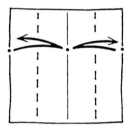

1 Add the quarter creases.

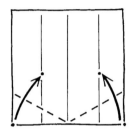

2 Starting at the center of the lower edge, fold either corner to touch the quarter creases (see next diagram). The accuracy of these creases determines the success of the design, so don't flatten until you are sure of the position.

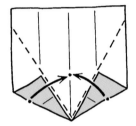

3 Take each folded edge to the center crease.

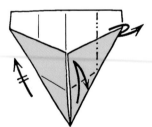

4 Two pre-creases; mountain fold the outer ¼ creases, valley the two existing smaller creases. This makes the next move much easier.

5 Study the creases carefully before starting. The mountain creases swing out to form new outside edges, the tip folds inward, flattening on the two valley creases (inside layers) and forming a new crease along the dotted line (lower layer) . . .

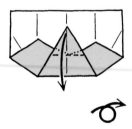

6 . . . like this. Fold the triangle down as far as it will go (without tearing) and turn over.

GLIDER

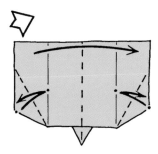

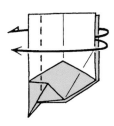

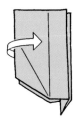

7 Enlarged view. Reinforce the two small creases (this helps step 11) and fold in half from left to right.

8 Swing either side over to form the wings. The creases begin where the side of the nose meets the horizontal edge and are parallel to the vertical edge.

9 Open out the first wing. The paper will be raised along the center.

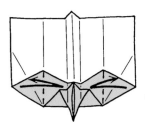

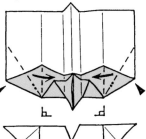

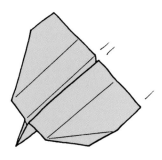

10 Creasing where shown, fold over on the original ¼ creases to transfer the crease to the upper layer.

11 Raise the outer corners to three dimensions using established creases. Arrange them as shown in the profile.

12 Ready for launch.

TOP VIEW

LAUNCHING POSITION

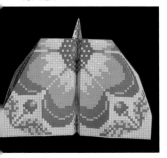

FLYING HINTS
This design has unusual flight characteristics since it begins with a loop before settling into a more conventional glide. Launch upward at about 45 degrees with moderate force. If you launch slightly harder, the glider will perform aerobatics.

DELTA GLIDER

LARRY HART

Many people seem to think that if you fold the front edge of a square over and form two wings, then the design will fly. It isn't until you have tried to create your own designs that you realize it isn't that simple. The secret of a good flier is balance, which the Delta Glider possesses.

Since the leading edge ends up with eight layers, you may need to start with thin paper until you are sure of the technique. Start with a square, colored side up, with both diagonals creased.

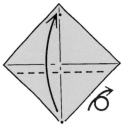

1 Fold one corner to touch a point just inside the opposite corner, about ⅛th of the diagonal. This distance isn't critical. Turn over.

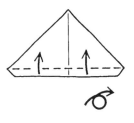

2 Fold over a double thickness on the horizontal diagonal crease. Turn back over again.

3 Take the inside edge to the folded edge and return, creasing only as far as the center crease.

4 Repeat the fold on the other side.

5 Using the last two creases and part of the diagonal, fold the paper into a "rabbit's ear", flattening the central flap to the left . . .

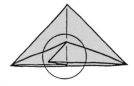

6 . . . like this. The circled section is enlarged from here on.

7 Take the loose corner of the triangular flap to the upper corner.

8 Fold the upper left edge of the triangular flap to the vertical edge and return. Open the paper out to step 7 again.

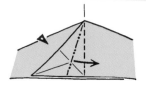

9 Squash the flap using (mostly) established creases . . .

DELTA GLIDER

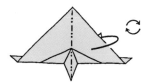

10 ... like this. Use established creases again to lift and flatten the lower corner into an inverted kite shape.

11 Make a mountain crease, parallel to the lower edge, that passes through the inside edge of the kite shape. The kite should open up into a diamond shape.

12 Fold the paper in half behind from right to left.

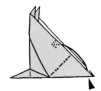

13 Make a crease at right angles to the raw edges that meets the lower end of the inside folded edge. Unfold.

14 Inside reverse fold the lower corner in between the wings.

15 Fold each wing down as far as it will comfortably go, then open them out to right angles.

LAUNCHING POSITION

FLYING HINTS
This design is best launched gently and level. If you launch it upward, it may swoop to one side and then level out. You can curl the ends of the wings slightly upward to improve stability.

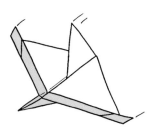

16 The Delta Glider.

DELTA GLIDER

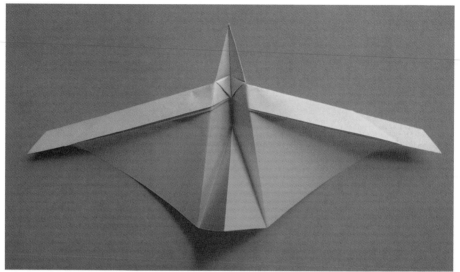

TOP VIEW

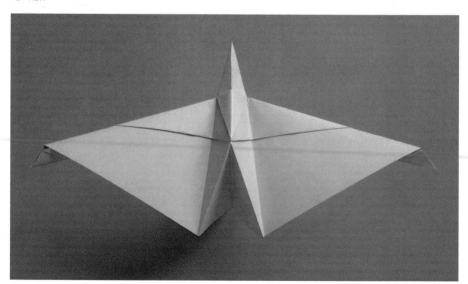

VIEW FROM BELOW

KENDAL FLIER

DAVID MITCHELL

This is one of the two designs in this book that utilizes the stored energy in a stretched elastic band to power the launch. This means the plane moves very fast and travels for very long distances, but has poor stability. For this reason it is best made from stiff paper. David hails from Kendal, hence the name.

Start with A4 paper, fold the long edges together, crease and unfold.

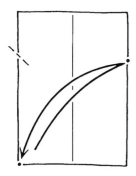

1 Take the nearest short edge to the right-hand long edge, but don't flatten. Instead, pinch the upper end of the fold to make a location crease.

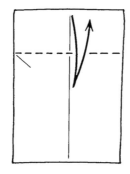

2 Make a valley fold through that location point, then unfold.

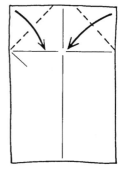

3 Fold the upper corners to lie along the horizontal crease.

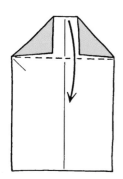

4 Refold along the crease made in step 2, then turn the paper over.

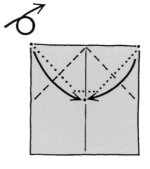

5 Take either end of the folded edge to the center point.

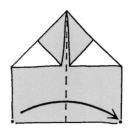

6 Fold in half from left to right.

KENDAL FLIER

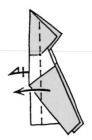

7 Fold the nose section in half, making the crease the full length of the paper. Repeat underneath, then open both sides out again.

8 Fold the wings down again, but make the paper fold underneath the layer at the nose.

9 Fold both wings down, making the crease pass through the location point shown.

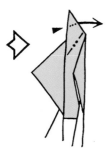

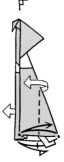

10 Enlarged view of the nose with the top wing lifted up slightly. Make an inside reverse fold (pre crease first if you wish), pushing the tip to the right . . .

11 . . . like this. Make a smaller outside reverse fold on the point (see the next diagram) and flatten the wing again. This forms the hook for the rubber band. Rotate the paper.

12 Make shaping creases on the wings, then open them up to 90 degrees.

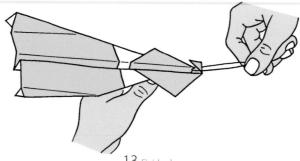

13 Finished.

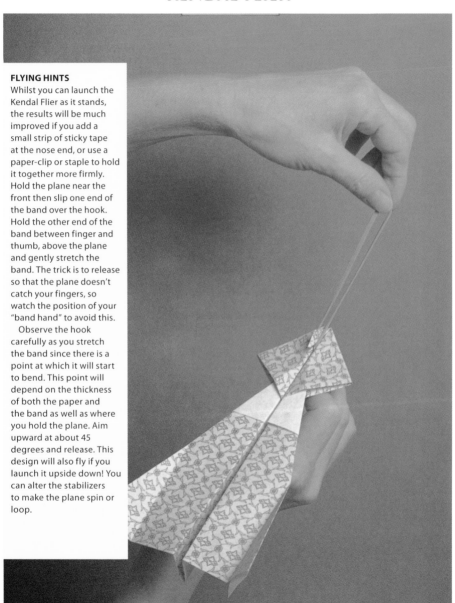

FLYING HINTS

Whilst you can launch the Kendal Flier as it stands, the results will be much improved if you add a small strip of sticky tape at the nose end, or use a paper-clip or staple to hold it together more firmly. Hold the plane near the front then slip one end of the band over the hook. Hold the other end of the band between finger and thumb, above the plane and gently stretch the band. The trick is to release so that the plane doesn't catch your fingers, so watch the position of your "band hand" to avoid this.

Observe the hook carefully as you stretch the band since there is a point at which it will start to bend. This point will depend on the thickness of both the paper and the band as well as where you hold the plane. Aim upward at about 45 degrees and release. This design will also fly if you launch it upside down! You can alter the stabilizers to make the plane spin or loop.

THE DAISY

NICK ROBINSON

This is a rare design because not only does it fly under the power of a rubber band, but it also works equally well as a hand-launched plane. The strength of the "hook" for the rubber band depends on the accuracy of the folds, the strength of the paper itself and exactly where you hold the plane. Once the technique for launching is mastered, you will be amazed how far and how high this design will fly. The design lends itself to many variations and step 4 is a good starting place for you to invent your own. "The Daisy" is named after my beautiful daughter.

Start with a sheet of strong A4 paper, colored side up. Add the vertical half-way crease.

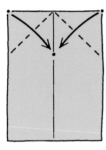

1 Fold two ends of the short edge to the center crease. turn the paper over.

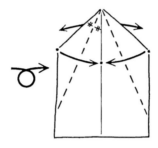

2 Take the folded edges to the center crease, allowing the corners to pop out from underneath.

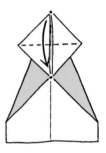

3 Fold the top corner of the square shape in half to the inside corner.

4 Fold each end of the upper folded edge to the inside corner of the triangle, then unfold.

5 Using the creases just made, fold the outside corners back in, but fold along the inside crease only so that the central (upside down) triangle is left as it is.

6 Convert the same crease to a mountain on the remaining flaps and fold them behind.

THE DAISY

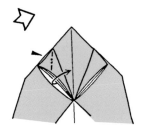

7 Lift up three of the four layers and fold them to the center crease, squashing into a kite shape.

8 Tuck the remaining half underneath, Repeat the last two steps on the other side.

9 Fold the narrow point upward.

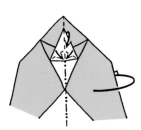

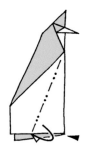

10 Make the point into a rabbit-ear (see the Basics of Folding chapter) and fold the plane in half behind.

11 Pre-crease the folded edge to the nearest raw edge.

12 Inside reverse on the crease you have just made.

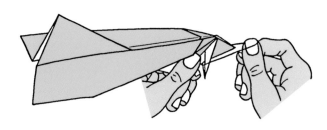

13 Fold either wing down between the location points shown.

14 Ready for launch.

THE DAISY

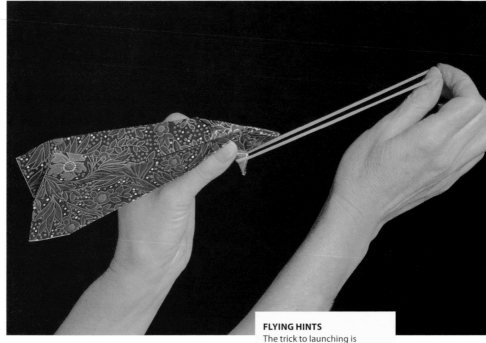

FLYING HINTS

The trick to launching is down to timing. You have to hold near the front end, tuck the band behind the hook and stretch it until it is tight. Depending on your folding, the paper and the band, there is a point where the hook will feel ready to bend. This is the time to release.

Experiment with timing and the tension of the band until you get it right. If you can't crack it and are getting desperate, add a staple or paper clip just behind the hook.

CHASSEUR

ALAIN GEORGEOT

The Chasseur or "Hunter" resembles some of the latest American and Russian fighter-bombers and looks very impressive in flight. It is also probably the most difficult project in the book, so please don't fold it until you have made most of the easier designs. The first four steps establish the diagonals. If you feel confident enough, fold them directly and start from step 5.

Make your first effort with a sheet of A4, then try a sheet of A5. The paper should be thin but not floppy. Start with the colored side down and fold the long half-way crease.

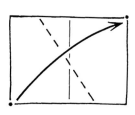

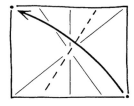

1 Take the bottom left corner to the top right and flatten.

2 Take one end of the folded edge to the other end, crease and unfold the paper completely.

3 Take the bottom right corner to the top left.

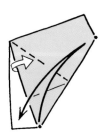
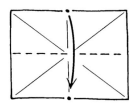
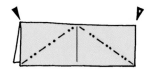

4 Again, crease and unfold completely.

5 You have now accurately established the diagonal creases. The two intermediate creases (steps 1 and 3) will not be omitted from the diagrams. Fold the paper in half.

6 Make the diagonal creases into mountains on either side, and inside reverse both halves of the folded edge. The creases are all there, but you will have to change three of them.

CHASSEUR

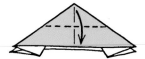

7 Fold the top corner in half downward.

8 Lift up the corner flap and the single layer beneath it and unfold them completely. The paper will not lie flat.

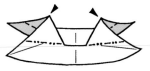

9 Squash both raised flaps carefully and neatly so they are symmetrical. Check this with the crease underneath.

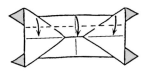

10 Fold the upper raw edge to the center.

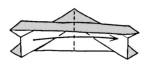

11 Fold in half from left to right and turn the paper round . . .

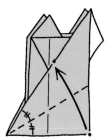

12 . . . to this position. Take the lower folded edge to the opposite side of the triangle.

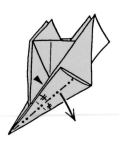

13 Carefully lift and squash the flap, checking that the layers inside have spread evenly; you might need to unfold the paper slightly and make the creases firmly.

14 Narrow the right-hand end of the squashed flap, then fold it in half.

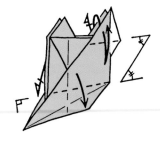

15 Fold both wings down between the two location points and open to right angles, and pre-crease two shaping creases on the wing-tips; the two creases should be parallel. Finally, shape the wings to match the profile below.

CHASSEUR

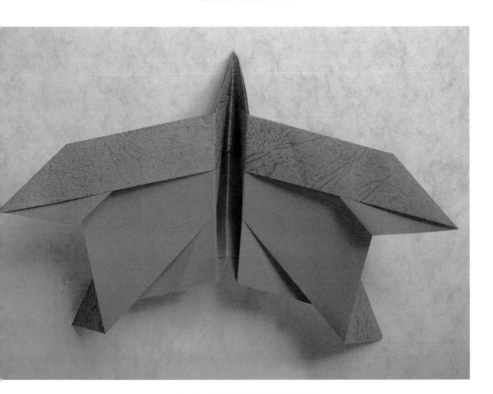

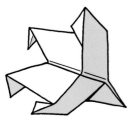

16 Congratulations! Now go back and make it again: it will be much neater.

FLYING HINTS
You have quite a few surfaces to adjust if you wish to experiment, but the basic design should be launched forward at a moderate speed. If you launch up upward, it will dive and loop. If the wings keep bending upward, making the Chasseur head downward, try using stiffer or thicker paper.

HARRIER

MICHAEL WEINSTEIN

Most paper airplanes depend upon concentrating weight at the front and the challenge is always to achieve this in an unusual and interesting way. This design uses a pleasing sequence of folds to produce a compact "locked" nose section which enables it to fly particularly well. The design isn't based on the British vertical take-off machine, says Michael!

The folding may look involved, but if you fold carefully and keep checking ahead to the next diagram, you will succeed. Make your creases firmly and try not to force the paper. As with all origami, continued folding will make things easier and you will begin to enjoy the moves.

Start with a sheet of A4, color side up, with the vertical center crease added.

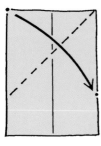

1 Fold the upper short edge to the right-hand long edge.

2 Fold the inside raw edge to the upper folded edge and return. Open the paper out again.

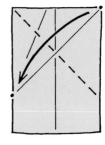

3 Repeat step one to the left-hand side.

4 Again, crease and return before opening out.

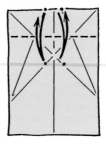

5 Using the location points shown, crease and return.

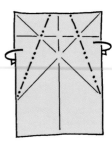

6 Mountain fold both sides behind on established creases, left corner first.

HARRIER

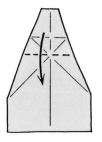

7 Fold the upper section down, making a crease through the intersection point of the three creases.

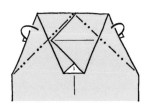

8 Fold the two corners behind.

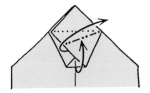

9 Open the pocket, swinging the flap upward. As you fold (slowly) the paper will flatten down naturally to produce the mountain crease. Try it and see! If your paper looks different from the diagram, check the order of the folds in step 6.

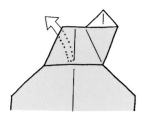

10 Open out the other hidden corner in the same way as the last step.

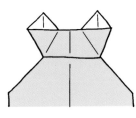

11 This is the result. Flatten the creases firmly and turn the paper over.

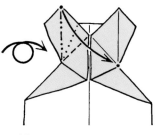

12 Using established creases, flatten the top left corner to the point shown. The dotted line shows the mountain crease that you flatten upon.

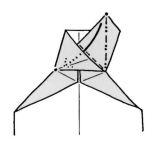

13 Step 12 created a small pocket; repeat the fold on the top right corner, tucking it within the pocket. Neat, isn't it?

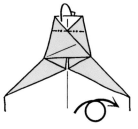

14 Fold the top edge behind, using the inside corner of the small triangle as a guideline. Turn over.

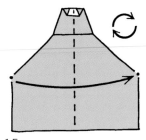

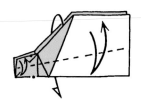

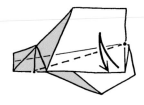

15 This is how the whole sheet looks now. Fold in half along the center crease from right to left.

16 Fold the upper side down, lining up the top and bottom edges of the nose-section. Unfold this side, then fold down behind and leave it down.

17 Make a crease that joins the right-hand end of the last crease with the lower edge of the nose section. Crease firmly and return.

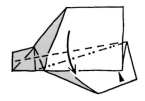

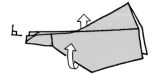

18 Inside reverse fold along the crease made in the last step, then fold the near-side wing down again.

19 Open the wings out to 90 degrees.

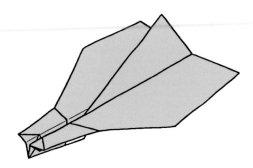

20 Ready for flight.

HARRIER

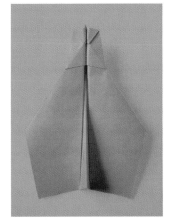

VIEW FROM BELOW

FLYING HINTS
The weight at the nose makes this a stable design that glides very well. Check the dihedral before flying and experiment with different speeds.

LAUNCHING POSITION

CHAPTER 6

AIRBORNE ORIGAMI

The appeal of flying paper doesn't end with darts and gliders. It provides endless fascination, including saucers, animals, spinners, even trays. Whilst you might expect a paper plane to fly, you would be surprised to see a flying elephant or Santa Claus! Each design has its own particular flying characteristics, some looping, some spinning; some may even nose-dive to the floor until you master the launching technique.

I hope this chapter will provide you with inspiration to create your own designs because it shows that almost anything can be made to fly given a bit of experimenting and improvising. Have fun!

WHEN I SEE AN ELEPHANT FLY

NICK ROBINSON

Inspired by the famous cartoon, this Elephant has particularly large ears, otherwise it wouldn't fly at all! The basis for the design is to fold half a "bird base" in origami terms and it was adapted from work by Frenchman Alain Georgeot.

Start with a square (grey or pink!), colored side down and add the center horizontal crease.

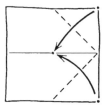

1 Fold both right-hand corners to the center crease.

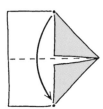

2 Fold the top edge in half downward.

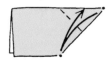

3 Crease the upper right corner to the lower right corner and return.

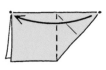

4 Fold the top right corner to the top left.

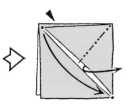

5 Using established creases, carefully squash the loose corner flat. . .

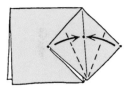

6 . . . to this position. Fold both lower sides of the squashed section to the vertical center crease.

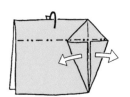

7 Mountain fold the top edge behind along the line formed by the horizontal inside edges of the kite shape. Open the flaps back out.

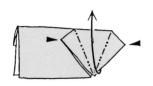

8 Fold the loose corner upward, gently pressing the sides in. . .

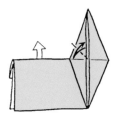

9 . . . to this position (as in the "Flapping Bird" steps 8 to 10). Pre-crease a small 45-degree fold on the diamond shape, then raise the hidden flap from behind.

WHEN I SEE AN ELEPHANT FLY

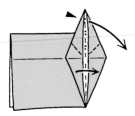 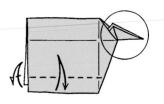 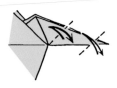

10 Add another 45-degree crease to match the last one, then use the creases shown to swing the paper across…

11 … into this position. Pre-crease two shaping folds on the raw edges. The circled area is enlarged in the next three diagrams.

12 Make two pre-creases at about 45 degrees.

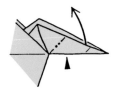  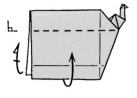

13 Use the larger to make an inside reverse fold.

14 Then repeat with the smaller crease to shape the end of the elephant's trunk.

15 Fold the wings to right angles and adjust the wingtips to match the profile shown below:

 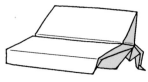

16 You can now see an elephant fly!

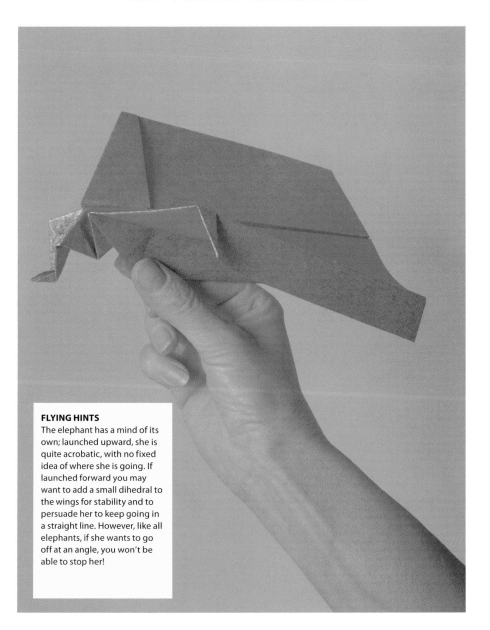

FLYING HINTS

The elephant has a mind of its own; launched upward, she is quite acrobatic, with no fixed idea of where she is going. If launched forward you may want to add a small dihedral to the wings for stability and to persuade her to keep going in a straight line. However, like all elephants, if she wants to go off at an angle, you won't be able to stop her!

HELICE

DIDIER BOURSIN

This design is one of many simple yet elegant folds by the editor of Le Pli, the magazine of the French Origami Society. Helice means "helix" or "spiral", both of which describe the beautiful spinning action of this design. The humble sycamore seed has provided inspiration for many spinning designs, yet few can match up to the aerodynamic perfection of nature. We can but try our best!

This design works best from smaller paper. Start with a 2:1 rectangle (half a square), colored side downward.

1 Fold both short edges to opposite long edges.

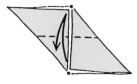

2 Crease in half from top to bottom.

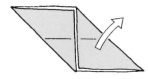

3 Open out the right-hand triangle.

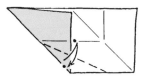

4 Fold the lower half of the folded edge to the horizontal crease and return.

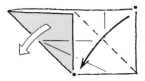

5 Fold the right-hand edge back in, then open out the left-hand triangle.

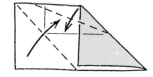

6 Fold the upper right corner in to the horizontal center crease (as in step 4), then fold the left-hand edge back in again.

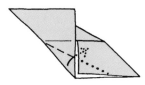

7 Put the fold made in step 4 back in, tucking it underneath the right-hand layer.

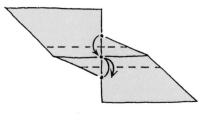

8 Pre-crease the lower valley fold, then crease the upper one.

HELICE

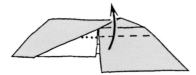

9 Fold the lower wing upward using the crease you have just made.

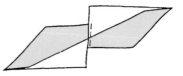

10 Make a gentle valley crease to raise the wings slightly, as in the profile shown below.

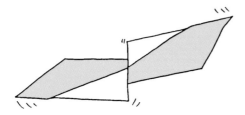

11 The Helice.

FLYING HINTS
The higher you can launch the Helice, the better chance it will have to work. Hold it gently in the center with the wings angled upward, then release it.

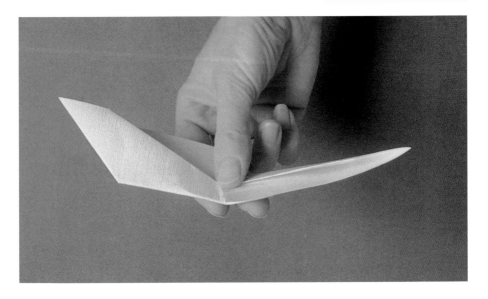

ONE-WAY TRAY

JOHN SMITH

This paper oddity doesn't fly in the conventional sense, but it has one fascinating property; no matter how you launch it, the One-Way Tray will always land the same way up! You can ask your friends to do their worst, but you will always be able to predict how it will land. The principle was discovered by John Smith and this design is my variation on his original tray. To make the final tray look sharp and clean, the bulk of the creases are put in before assembly.

Start with a square, colored side down, with both diagonals creased.

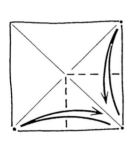

1 Fold in half both ways, but only crease half the width each time. Turn over.

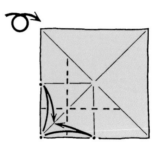

2 Add the quarter creases, again only creasing where shown.

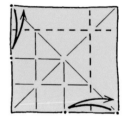

3 Add the remaining two creases across the full width.

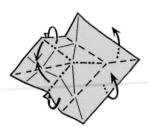

4 Start to collapse the paper using the creases shown. You will have to change the diagonal crease in places. Take your time and try not to force the paper.

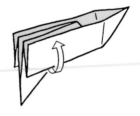

5 This is the result. Open out the first flap.

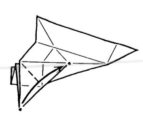

6 Fold the lower corner to the center point.

ONE-WAY TRAY

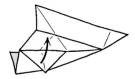 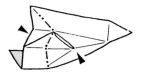 

7 Swing the triangular flap to lie flat.

8 Make the fold triangular by making the existing crease into a from corner to corner.

9 . . . like this. Sharpen all the creases and turn the paper over.

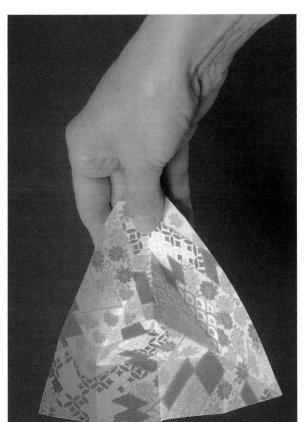 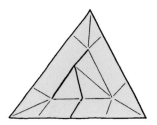

10 Here is your One-Way tray.

FLYING HINTS
None: just release it from as high a place as possible.

HEPTAD RING

JEFF BAYNON

Jeff is a designer of origami who works exclusively with the combinations and possibilities of geometrically derived crease patterns. This can produce fascinating results such as this ring.

The Heptad Ring, whilst not designed with flight in mind, certainly makes an eye-catching and attractive pattern as it spins through the air.

You need seven squares, preferably with different and bright colors on either side. Paper-backed foil is ideal because it has more weight than ordinary paper; you could even laminate (glue) two different colored sheets together.

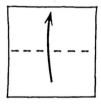

1 Fold in half upward.

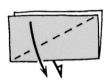

2 Make a crease that joins the left-hand end of the folded edge with the right-hand edge of the first upper edge. You can of course produce a mirror-image copy by reversing these creases from left to right and vice versa, but all seven units must be identical. Make six more "Units".

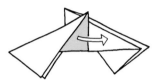

3 Slide two units together …

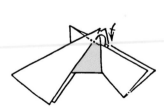

4 … as far as they will comfortably go. Lock the units together by folding the two loose tips on either side within. Join all seven units in the same way.

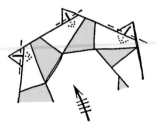

5 Lock further by folding the single tips into the pockets as well.

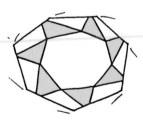

6 Complete.

HEPTAD RING

FLYING HINTS
Hold the ring like a frisbee so that the side furthest from your hand is raised to an angle of about 30 degrees to the horizontal.

Release with a flick of the wrist. The secret of a level flight is to impart as much spin to the ring as possible, but do not throw too quickly or it will turn over in flight.

BOOMERANG

MAX HULME

Boomerangs are beautifully curved pieces of wood, but we can make a working version from a rectangle of paper. This design is different from all the others in this book because every crease is at 45 or 90 degrees. The sequence is logical and efficient if you crease accurately.

This boomerang uses a 2:1 rectangle (half a square), but it will work from other similar rectangles, such as bank cheques. The paper needs to be crisp, but not too thick. Start with the colored side down and crease the short side into quarters.

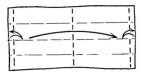

1 Fold each short edge over a little way, crease firmly and unfold. Fold the paper in half from left to right.

2 Take each corner of the folded edge to meet the outside quarter crease and return. Open the paper back out.

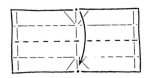

3 Fold the upper long edge to the lower.

4 Pre-crease a valley.

5 Then make an inside reverse fold using the crease you have just made.

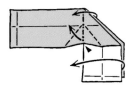

6 Using established creases (you will need to alter the direction of a few) swing the right-hand flap to the left, raising a small triangular flap.

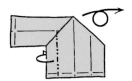

7 Fold the quarter flap underneath, tucking the top end inside the triangular pocket. Turn the paper over.

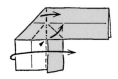

8 Repeat step 6 on this side, again raising a small triangular flap.

9 Tuck the upper layer within, unfolding the triangular flap inside. The next three steps show an enlargement of the circled area.

BOOMERANG

10 Fold the left corner to the crease (made in step 1) and unfold.

11 Mountain fold the small strip underneath, allowing the corner to fold in naturally on established creases.

12 This is the result.

13 Fold the layer within.

14 Lock the end by tucking the small flap within the closed pocket. It is easiest to start with the square end, then the angled end. Flatten firmly. Turn over.

15 Then repeat steps 13 and 14, locking the other end.

16 Then repeat steps 13 and 14 locking the other end.

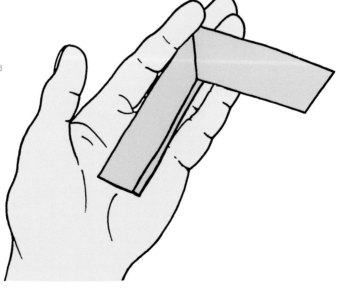

BOOMERANG

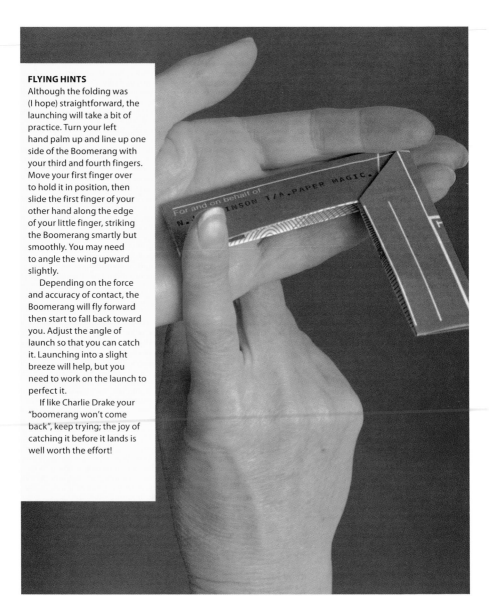

FLYING HINTS

Although the folding was (I hope) straightforward, the launching will take a bit of practice. Turn your left hand palm up and line up one side of the Boomerang with your third and fourth fingers. Move your first finger over to hold it in position, then slide the first finger of your other hand along the edge of your little finger, striking the Boomerang smartly but smoothly. You may need to angle the wing upward slightly.

Depending on the force and accuracy of contact, the Boomerang will fly forward then start to fall back toward you. Adjust the angle of launch so that you can catch it. Launching into a slight breeze will help, but you need to work on the launch to perfect it.

If like Charlie Drake your "boomerang won't come back", keep trying; the joy of catching it before it lands is well worth the effort!

FLYING SAUCER

NICK ROBINSON

Although flying saucers are generally circular, we can make an impressive version using a square. This is easily converted into an octagon, then into a heptagon as we make the paper three-dimensional. All the creases are easily located, providing you take your time. Because it is launched with a spin, this design uses gyroscopic principles rather than those of conventional paper airplanes. The design was inspired by a saucer made from a circular piece of paper.

Start with a brightly colored piece of paper, the heavier the better; you might even use thin card. Foil-backed paper also works very well. From the white side, crease in half and from corner to corner both ways. Make all these folds valleys and keep it white side up.

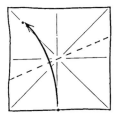

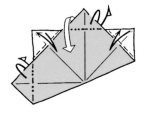

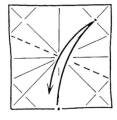

1 Making sure the crease passes through the center of the paper, take the lower center-point to lie along the upper left diagonal . . .

2 . . . like this. Pre-crease the corner along the edges in front (valleys) and below (mountains). Open the paper back out.

3 Repeat step 1 to the right-hand side and unfold.

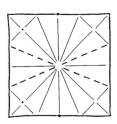

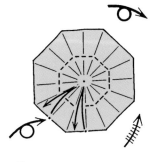

4 This is the crease pattern so far. Repeat step 1 twice more using the location marks shown to complete the radial creases.

5 Fold each corner to the creases made in step 2, then over again using the crease itself. Turn the paper over.

6 The paper should now be octagonal in shape. Fold the center of each edge to the center point, but only crease between either adjacent diagonals before opening. Turn over again.

FLYING SAUCER

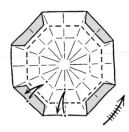

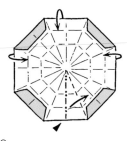

7 Fold each edge to the "spoke" creases you have just made, creasing again only between the diagonals. Then unfold.

8 Make one crease into a mountain, then pleat it sideways, raising the sides of the paper to form a central hollow. The paper is three dimensional from here onward.

9 Lock the pleat by folding the outer edge to the diagonal, then folding over using the diagonal.

FLYING HINTS
Launch the saucer like a frisbee, trying to impart as much spin as possible at the launch by "flicking" your wrist. Raise the opposite edge to your hand upward slightly.

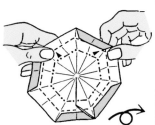

10 Lift the paper up and gently press it into shape using the creases you have made. Go slowly and try not to force the paper. Turn the paper over; it should match the profile below.

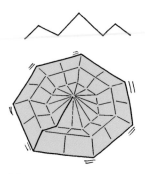

11 It came from outer space!

ROCKET

This is a fold that was taught to (and remembered by) American folder Shawn Truitt when he was a child. The folding sequence may at first appear complex, but will soon become straightforward with practice and you can then enjoy the exciting and interesting moves such as steps 3, 9, 14 and 23, as well as the beautiful arrangement in step 22.

Use slightly heavier paper than normal, but not so thick that you cannot crease accurately. It will work well made from foil-backed paper. Start with a square, colored side down.

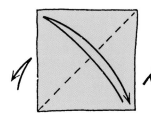

1 Crease both diagonals firmly and turn the paper over.

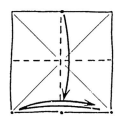

2 Crease in half from side to side, then fold the top edge to the nearest edge.

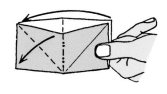

3 All the creases you need are in place, so gently swing the left hand side over to flatten on top of the right hand side. This should happen quite naturally..

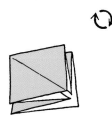

4 This is the result. Turn the paper so the corner where the four points meet is nearest to you.

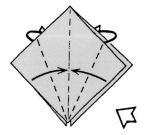

5 Fold a flap toward the center crease on the left and right hand side to form a kite shape. Repeat underneath.

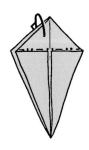

6 Fold the triangular flap behind.

ROCKET

 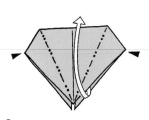 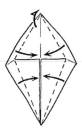

7 Open the two flaps back out.

8 Making sure the paper is flat on the table, lift up the first layer at the near-side corner and open up a pocket.

9 Keep lifting and swinging the point away from you and begin to fold the sides in, using the valley creases shown. The lower flaps will already be valleys but you will have to alter the direction of the upper ones.

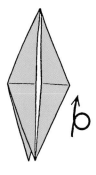 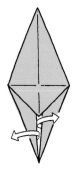 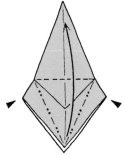

10 This is the result. The move is known as a "petal fold". Turn the paper over.

11 Open out the flaps from beneath the triangular flap.

12 Repeat steps 8 to 10 on this side, swinging the triangular flap upward. Turn the resulting shape upside down.

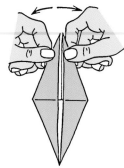 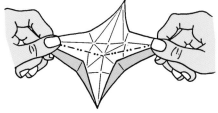

13 The two loose points should be on top. Hold one in each hand and slowly pull apart . . .

14 . . . until the paper opens up.. You are trying to persuade the central crease to pop up into a continuous mountain crease, so keep gently moving the points apart . . .

ROCKET

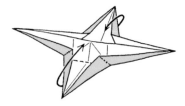

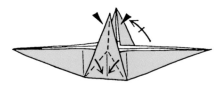

15 ...There it goes! Flatten the two side points inward, allowing them to flatten into a natural position ...

16 ...like this. Make a rabbit's ear fold on each flap, flattening them to the right.

17 Open the first half of the paper out and flatten.

18 Fold the right side across to the left on the half-way crease.

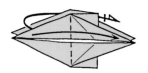

19 Fold both long points in half to the right.

20 Make another rabbit's ear fold on either side in the same way as step 16. Fold the nearside flap down, the other one upward.

21 Swing the lower half back into view, flattening the upper horizontal point to the left.

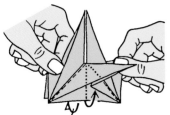

22 This should be the result. If; not, rearrange the flaps to match. Fold the top section in half behind, allowing the lower point to rise...

23 ...to this position. Press the sides slowly together, encouraging the vertical center crease to spread apart on either side. You are forming a small "preliminary base". Follow the creases carefully, repeating behind and the flaps will point in different directions.

ROCKET

 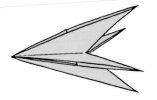

24 This is the result. Moving anti-clockwise, fold each of the lower flaps within the pocket of the larger points. This locks the design together.

25 Complete.

FLYING HINTS

Hold the Rocket toward the front end by a single layer and launch it high into the air as fast as you can. You need to experiment with the angle of launch (trajectory) to get the maximum distance. If you make a target on the floor you could play darts with the Rocket.

HELICOPTER

NICK ROBINSON

There is a well-known "twirling" toy made from a strip of paper with one end cut down the middle and the two flaps bent outward. The bent wings cause the Helicopter to spin round as it falls. This is a folded version of the same principle. Many folders have produced designs similar to this one, which is based on a traditional design for a sailboat independently created by Makoto Yamaguchi. Choose a paper that is fairly thin, but not too floppy. Start with a square, colored side up.

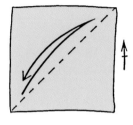

1 Crease both diagonals and turn over.

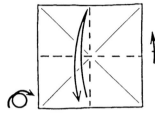

2 Fold in half both ways.

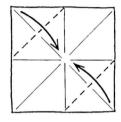

3 Fold two opposite corners to the center.

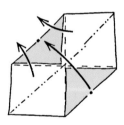

4 Using the creases shown, collapse the paper.

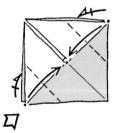

5 Fold both outside corners (upper layer only) to the center.

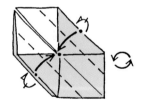

6 Narrow the flaps by folding to the center again. Repeat steps 5 to 6 on the other side. Turn the paper round slightly.

HELICOPTER

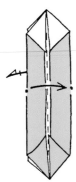

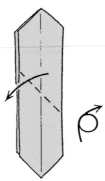

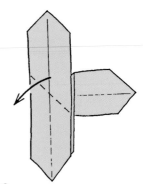

7 Fold the upper left-hand flap in half to the right. Repeat the fold underneath. This move is known in America as a "minor miracle".

8 Swing the top layer down and to the left at 45 degrees. Make sure the crease passes through the center (where the hidden layer inside lies). There are quite a few layers so press firmly. Turn over.

9 Repeat step 8 on this side.

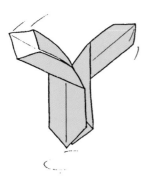

10 The finished Helicopter.

FLYING HINTS

The amount of spin caused by the wings depends on the angle that you bend them to. This in turn depends on the flexibility of the paper used. Launch the Helicopter either by throwing it high in the air or by dropping it from as high up as possible.

FLYING SANTA

PAUL JACKSON

This design is unusual in that it requires two sheets. Paul is a well-respected creator and author who prefers to keep his folds simple and accessible. This design could have been made from a single sheet, but would have involved a lot of complicated and ugly folding. By using two sheets the design is much cleaner and easier.

Start with two sheets of light-weight paper, preferably red and white on opposite sides. Both sheets start with the colored side upward. Add a diagonal crease and make a small pinch-mark to locate the center.

BODY

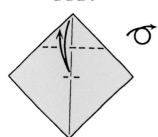

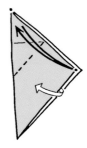

1 Fold one end of the crease to the center and return. Turn the paper over.

2 Fold in half along the diagonal crease.

3 Fold the top corner to the other end of the raw edge and return. Unfold the paper.

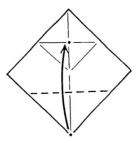

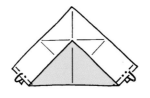

4 Take the bottom corner to the ¼ crease.

5 Fold a small strip behind on either side.

6 Pre-crease two valleys along the inside edges.

FLYING SANTA

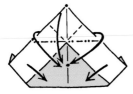

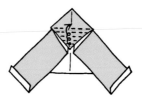

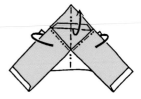

7 Use established creases to swing the top corner downward, bringing all the location points together.

8 Fold the lower corner of the small square over and over, the last fold being a diagonal. This forms the lining to Santa's hood.

9 Emphasize the creases shown, letting the hood swing open . . .

10 . . . until the paper looks like this. Unfold the last step.

LEGS
Take the other square (colored side up) and fold the vertical crease.

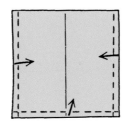

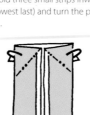

11 Fold three small strips inward (the lowest last) and turn the paper over . . .

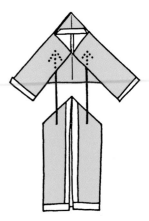

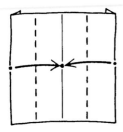

12 Fold two sides to the center crease.

13 Mountain fold the top two corners behind to the center crease, finishing the legs.

14 Slide the leg section within the body, as far as it will go.

FLYING SANTA

15 Re-form the creases made in step 9, adding them to the leg section inside. Open the hood out slightly and adjust to the position shown in the profile.

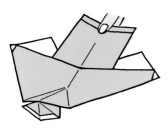

16 Santa ready for his rounds.

FLYING HINTS

Do not throw Santa, but gently release him forward at a slight angle and he will glide gracefully to the floor. If you fold this design from black and white paper, you can make a flying nun!

SKY-FLYING BUTTERFLY

YOSHIHIDE MOMOTANI

Yoshihide is one of Japan's master-folders and has written many books on the subject. Along with his talented family, he travels all over the world teaching and displaying his superb exhibits. The design here starts with a series of apparently unpromising pleats to produce a butterfly that swoops, dives and loops.

Start with a 6 in (15 cm) square of thin and suitably attractive paper, color side down. Crease the vertical center fold.

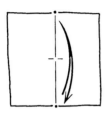

1 Gently pinch the center point of the crease.

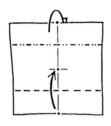

2 Valley fold the lower side to the center mark, repeat behind with the upper side.

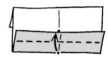

3 Take the lower folded edge to the center.

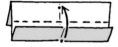

4 Take the lower edge upward to leave the same gap below the folded edge as above it. Note that this crease is not a center crease. Check the next diagram for help.

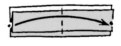

5 Fold in half from left to right.

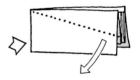

6 Enlarged view. Gently pull out the upper single layer to the position shown in the next diagram. The new crease meets the right-hand edge where two hidden edges meet . . .

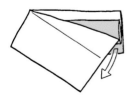

7 . . . like this. Repeat on the other side.

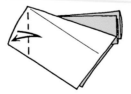

8 Pre-crease along a hidden vertical edge.

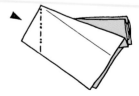

9 Now push the triangle inside, making a reverse fold. It doesn't matter which side of the inner layer it goes.

SKY-FLYING BUTTERFLY

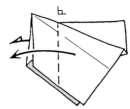

10 Fold both wings over, making a vertical crease starting at the angle change on the top edge. Open them out to right angles.

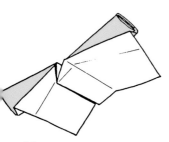

11 The Sky-Flying Butterfly ready for flight.

FLYING HINTS
Because the paper is very light, it is easily affected by air currents. This results in an unpredictable flight pattern, very much in keeping with a real butterfly. Launch at almost any angle or speed.

LAUNCHING POSITION

VIEW FROM BELOW

MOTH

NICK ROBINSON

Starting with the classic folding sequence for the Hawk Dart, Snub-nosed Delta and others, the Moth has two antennae which can be shaped for extra realism.

This design can be made from almost any shaped rectangle. Start with the colored side down, fold in half width-wise and open.

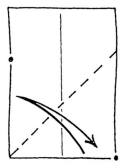

1 Fold the nearest short edge to the left hand edge, crease firmly and return.

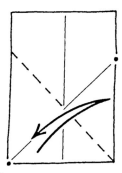

2 Repeat to the right-hand side.

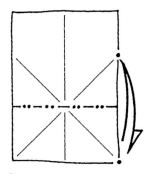

3 Add a mountain crease which passes through the intersection of the valley creases. (it is easiest to turn over and make a valley.)

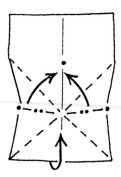

4 Press in the center of the creases. The sides of the mountain crease should "pop" upward. Using the creases you have made, swing the three lower dotted points toward the upper one.

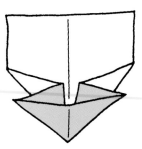

5 This is the half-way stage.

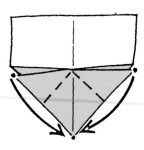

6 Fold the loose point on either side down to the lower corner.

MOTH

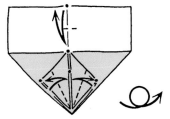

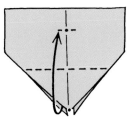

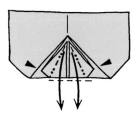

7 Mark the half-way point of the upper single layer. Fold the lower edges of the small square to the vertical center, crease and return. Turn the paper over.

8 Take the lower corner (all layers) to meet the location point made in the last step.

9 Using established creases, swing the two inside corners down, pressing gently on either side until they flatten into a diamond shape.

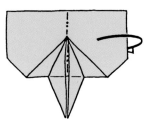

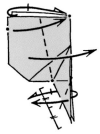

10 Mountain in half from right to left.

11 Fold the lower points over (check the next diagram) to form the antennae. Valley fold both wings out; the crease starts at the lower inside corner, the left-hand edge just touches the right-hand upper corner.

12 This is the result; open out the upper wing, then fold the antennae to point the opposite way.

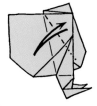

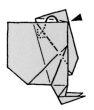

13 Make a pre-crease as shown; the upper end meets the wing crease, the lower end is as far as the paper will comfortably go.

14 Inside reverse along the crease you have just made.

15 Adjust both wings to right-angles and rotate the paper to a horizontal position.

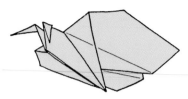

16 The Moth.

TOP VIEW

VIEW FROM BELOW

LAUNCHING POSITION

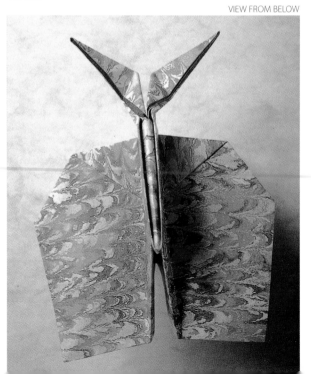

FLYING HINTS

Because of the antennae, this design is very sensitive to the speed of launching. Hold it in front of you and push gently forward. Too fast and the Moth will stall. Alter the antennae for different effects; having them at different angles will make the Moth rotate in flight.

FLAPPING BIRD

This traditional design has delighted both children and adults for many years. Whilst not an airplane, it flies magnificently in your hand. Once you have learnt this design, be prepared to make one at the drop of a hat because everyone will want one!

The "flapper" has been made from 16 ft (5 m) paper right down to a square ⅛ in (2.9 mm) across, so there is plenty of scope. There is a bit of a knack to making it flap properly, so be patient. Start with a square, colored side down.

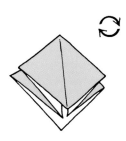

1 Crease both diagonals firmly and turn the paper over.

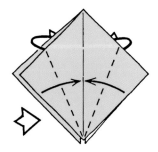

2 Crease in half from side to side, then fold the top edge to the nearest edge.

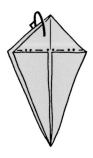

3 All the creases you need are in place, so gently swing the left-hand side over to flatten on top of the right-hand side. This happens very naturally if you have creased carefully.

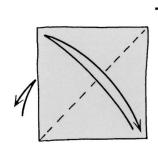

4 This is the result, known in the origami world as a preliminary base. There are many other ways of arriving at this fold. Turn the paper so the corner where the four points meet points toward you (this is important).

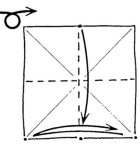

5 Fold a flap toward the center crease on the left and right-hand side to form a kite shape. Repeat underneath.

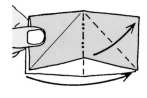

6 Fold the triangular flap behind.

FLAPPING BIRD

 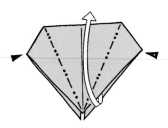 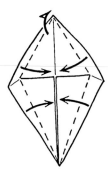

7 Open the two flaps back out.

8 Making sure the paper is flat on the table, lift up the first layer at the near-side corner and open up a pocket.

9 Keep lifting and swinging the point away from you and begin to fold the sides in using the valley creases shown. The lower flaps will already be valleys, the upper ones will need to be carefully altered.

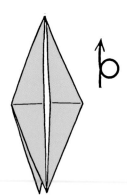 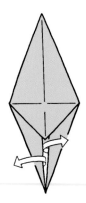 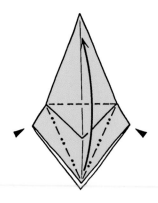

10 This is the result. The move is known as a "petal fold". Turn the paper over.

11 Open out the flaps from beneath the triangular flap.

12 Repeat steps 8 to 10 on this side, swinging the triangular flap upward.

FLAPPING BIRD

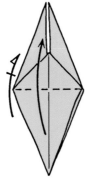

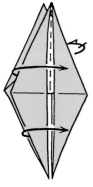

13 You should have a neat diamond shape on either side. Fold the upper right-hand side over to the left. Turn the paper over and repeat on the other side.

14 The two loose flaps now start within the kite shape. Fold the lower point upward to meet them. Repeat on the other side.

15 Hold one of the hidden flaps and pull it out, allowing the paper to swing out at the bottom.

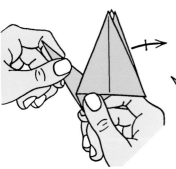

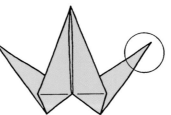

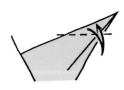

16 When the flap is in the approximate position shown, flatten the base of the paper with your other hand. Repeat the last two steps with the other hidden flap, trying to make the angles match.

17 Almost finished. The next three diagrams, showing how to make the head, are an enlargement of the circled area.

18 Fold over the tip of the pointed flap, crease firmly and unfold it.

19 Then push the paper in to make an inside reverse fold . . .

20 . . . like this.

FLAPPING BIRD

FLYING HINTS
Try to curl the wings forward and downward toward the lower front corner. Some folders put a crease here, but that destroys the beautiful curved action. When the wings begin to curl, hold the bird at the lower front corner and mid-way along the tail, then slowly pull the tail in the direction in which it points. The wings will begin to bend stiffly forward, then as the bird "learns", they will move more smoothly and with luck, elegantly!

19 The bird is finished, but you need to teach it how to fly!

BIBLIOGRAPHY

There are many books on the market that include some paper airplanes, mostly the well-known designs. The majority of these, however, include much cutting and glueing which seems to me to be contrary to the simplicity and elegance of purely folded designs. This list is not a comprehensive one, but includes the best folding-only (with the odd exception) books currently in print.

BARNABY, RALPH. *How to Make and Fly Paper Aeroplanes* (Four Winds Press)
COLLINS, JOHN. *The Gliding Flight* (Ten Speed Press)
HUI, EDMOND. *Fold It, Fly It* (Patrick Stephens Ltd) [entitled *Amazing Paper Planes in the US*; (St Martin's Press)]

LAUX, KEITH. *The World's Greatest Paper Airplane and Toy Book* (Tub Books Inc)
MOMOTANI, YOSHIHIDE. *Sora Tobu Tori no Origami (Origami Birds Flying in the Sky)* Seinbundo Shinko Sha (In Japanese, but with clear diagrams.)
MORRIS, CAMPBELL. *Advanced Paper Aircraft Construction* Volumes 1, 2 and 3 (Angus & Robertson) [Vols. 1 & 2 appear in the US as *The Best Paper Aircraft* (Putnam Publishing Group)]
NAKAMURA, EIJI. *Flying Origami* (Japan Publications); *Origami Airplanes* (Japan Publications)
PAVARIN, FRANCO. *Aerei, Jet ed Astronaui Di Carta Volanti* (Il Castello)
WEISS, STEPHEN. *Wings & Things; Origami that Flies* (St Martin's Press)

ADDRESSES

If you have enjoyed the folds in this book, you are strongly recommended to get in touch with the nearest Origami Society. Any such society will publish a magazine and have access to unusual paper, origami books and local contacts with whom you can share ideas and folds.

AMERICA
Friends of the Origami
Centre of America
15 West 77th Street
New York City
NY 10024

BELGIUM
B.N.O.S.
Postbus 100
B–2400 Mol

ENGLAND
British Origami Society
253 Park Lane
Poynton
Stockport SK12 1RH

FRANCE
Mouvement Français des Plieurs de Papier
56 Rue Coiolis
75012 Paris

GERMANY
Origami Deutschland
Postfach 1630
8050 Freising

ITALY
Centro Diffusione Origami
Castella Postale 225
40100 Bologna

Centro Italiano Origami
PO Box 357
10100 Torino

JAPAN
International Origami Centre
PO Box 3
Ogikubo
Tokyo

Nippon Origami Association
1–096 Domir Gobancho
12 — gobancho
Chiyoda Ku
Tokyo 102

SPAIN
Associacion Espanola de Papiroflexia
C/Pedro Teixeira 9
ESC IZO–9 DCHA
2020 Madrid

INDEX

ACKNOWLEDGEMENTS

The route to this book was made easier by Mark Kennedy, Michael Weinstein and David Venables, to whom go my grateful thanks.

To all the contributors who freely gave their creations, assistance and unselfish advice, my thanks: John Smith, Didier Boursin, Dr James Sakoda, Yoshihide Momotani, Michael Weinstein, Mark Kennedy, Stephen Weiss, Francis Ow, Paul Jackson, Max Hulme, Edwin Corrie, Alain Georgeot, Larry Hart, Jeff Beynon, Carlos Gonzalez Garcia, David Mitchell, Kunihiko Kasahara, Charles Peck and David Lister.

The paper for the folded examples came from Minako Ishibashi, the Sheffield Scrap Store, Whiteheads Craft Centre, G. F. Smith & Son (Hull), B.O.S. Supplies and Fairleigh Post Office. Thank you also to the Play Resources Centre for liberal use of their photocopier.

As with the general area of origami creativity, many paper designs follow similar lines and it is probable that some of the folds in this book have (unknown to me) been independently created by other folders. If this is the case, either contact me through the publishers or look on it as a case of "great minds thinking alike". I would love to see other folders' designs. Please send them via the British Origami Society address.

Thanks also to the wonderful members of the British Origami Society who stoked my interest in origami into a blazing fire: Mick Guy, Dave Brill, Wayne Brown (who diligently checked my diagrams), Paul Jackson and countless others.

Most of all, thanks to my wife Alison for her love and patience and to my beautiful Daisy and little Nick for "testing" the designs and keeping out of my way.